WORKING PAPERS FOR EXERCISES AND PROBLEMS

VOLUME 1: CHAPTERS 1–18 AND APPENDIXES A–C

PRINCIPLES OF ACCOUNTING

2005e

Belverd E. Needles, Jr.
DePaul University

Marian Powers
Northwestern University

Susan V. Crosson
Santa Fe Community College, Florida

HOUGHTON MIFFLIN COMPANY BOSTON NEW YORK

Senior Sponsoring Editor: Bonnie Binkert
Senior Development Editor: Margaret M. Kearney
Project Editor: Claudine Bellanton
Senior Manufacturing Coordinator: Priscilla J. Bailey
Marketing Manager: Todd Berman

Copyright © 2005 by Houghton Mifflin Company. All rights reserved.

No part of this work may be reproduced or transmitted in any form or by any means, electronic or mechanical, including photocopying or recording, or by any information storage or retrieval system without the prior written permission of Houghton Mifflin Company unless such copying is expressly permitted by federal copyright law. Address inquiries to College Permissions, Houghton Mifflin Company, 222 Berkeley Street, Boston, MA 02116-3764.

Printed in the U.S.A.

ISBN: 0-618-37992-4

56789-CRS-07

NOTE TO STUDENTS

This book contains Working Papers to be used in preparing solutions to all Exercises and Problems, and selected cases in Chapters 1–18 and Appendixes A–C of *Principles of Accounting*, 2005e. The Working Papers are designed to simplify your work; appropriate forms for computational assignments for each exercise and problem are provided, and some preliminary information has been printed to get you started. We have added some blank forms at the end of the Working Papers for those who need to start over or who may want to rework some of the exercises or problems for additional practice.

We have occasionally provided hints on the placement of data. This is usually done only once on a page. Students can infer from these hints where to enter subsequent data on that page so that it can be displayed and calculated correctly.

Accounting Format Guide

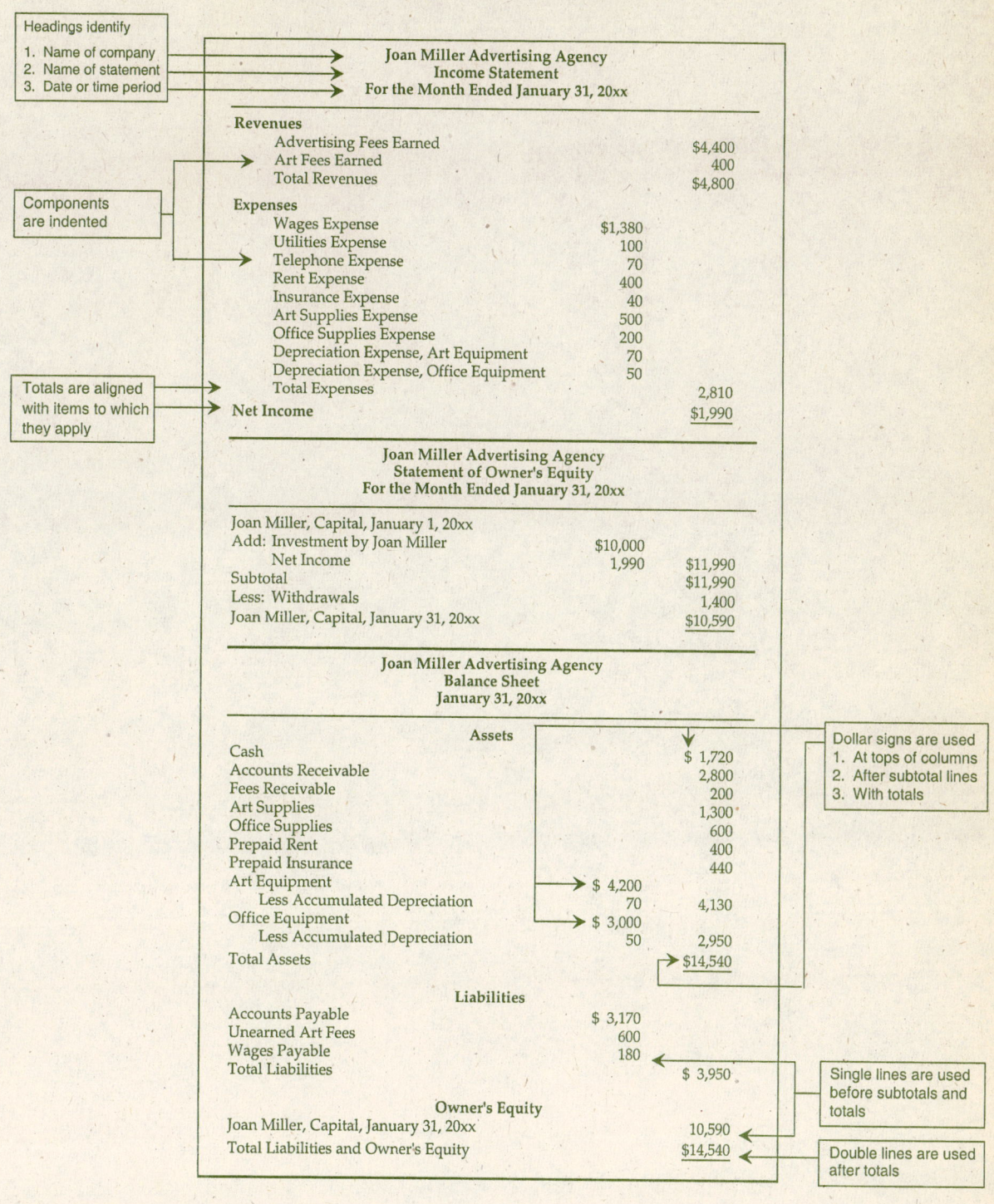

Chapter 1, SE 1.

1.		4.	
2.		5.	
3.			

Chapter 1, SE 2.

1.		4.	
2.		5.	
3.		6.	

Chapter 1, SE 3.

1.	Assets	=	
2.	Owner's Equity	=	
3.	Liabilities	=	

Chapter 1, SE 4.

1.		Assets	=	Liabilities	+	Owner's Equity
			=		+	Owner's Equity
			−		=	
		Owner's Equity	=			
2.		Assets	=			
			=			
			=			
			=			
			=			
		Liabilities	=			

Chapter 1, SE 5.

1.	Beginning:			=	
			Liabilities	=	
				=	
	Change:				
				=	
	End:		Owner's Equity	=	
2.	Beginning:			=	
			Assets	=	
				=	
	Change:				
				=	
	End:		Owner's Equity	=	

Chapter 1, SE 6.

1. Net income =

2. Net income =

3. Net income =

Chapter 1, SE 7.

Net income =

Chapter 1, SE 8.

	Assets	Liabilities	Owner's Equity
1.	+	+	NC
2.			
3.			
4.			
5.			
6.			

Chapter 1, SE 9.

	Assets	Liabilities	Owner's Equity
1.			
2.			
3.			
4.			
5.			
6.			

Chapter 1, SE 10.

Anatole Company
Balance Sheet
June 30, 20x1

Assets		Liabilities	
		Owner's Equity	
Total assets		Total liabilities and owner's equity	

Chapter 1, E 1.

1.	5.	9.
2.	6.	10.
3.	7.	11.
4.	8.	12.

Chapter 1, E 2.

People who are interested in Vylex's financial statements are the following:

Chapter 1, E 3.

1.
2.
3.
4.

Chapter 1, E 4.

1.	6.
2.	7.
3.	8.
4.	9.
5.	10.

Chapter 1, E 5.

Company	Sales
Inchip	
Wong	
Mitzu	
Works	

Company	Assets
Inchip	
Wong	
Mitzu	
Works	

_____ is the largest in terms of sales.
_____ is the largest in terms of assets.

Chapter 1, E 6.

1.		Assets	=	Liabilities	+	Owner's Equity
			=			
		Liabilities	=			
2.		Assets	=			
			=			
		Assets	=			
3.		Assets	=			
			=			
		Assets	=			
		Liabilities	=			
4.	Beginning:		=			
			=			
			=			
	Change:					
			=			
	End:	Owner's Equity	=			

Chapter 1, E 7.

a.		d.		g.	
b.		e.		h.	
c.		f.			

Chapter 1, E 8.

	Assets	Liabilities	Owner's Equity	
a.				
b.				
c.				
d.				
e.				
f.				
g.				
h.				
i.				
j.				

Chapter 1, E 9.

1.
2.
3.
4.
5.

Chapter 1, E 10.

1. Net income (loss) is:

	Assets	=	Liabilities	+	Owner's Equity
End:		=		+	
Beginning:		=		+	
Net income (loss)					

2. Net income (loss) is:

Change in Owner's Equity	
+ Owner's withdrawal	
Net income (loss)	

3. Net income (loss) is:

Change in Owner's Equity	
− Owner's investment	
Net income (loss)	

4. Net income (loss) is:

Change in Owner's Equity	
+ Owner's withdrawal	
− Owner's investment	
Net income (loss)	

Chapter 1, E 11.

1.		2.	
a.		a.	
b.		b.	
c.		c.	
d.		d.	
e.		e.	
f.		f.	
g.		g.	

Chapter 1, E 12.

Solos Company
Balance Sheet
December 31, 20xx

Assets		Liabilities	
		Owner's Equity	
Total assets		Total liabilities and owner's equity	

Chapter 1, E 13.

Income Statement	Set A		Set B		Set C	
Revenues	$1,100			(g)	$340	
Expenses		(a)	5,200			(m)
Net income		(b)		(h)	$180	
Statement of Owner's Equity						
Beginning balance	$2,900		$15,400		$200	
Net income		(c)	1,600			(n)
Less withdrawals	200			(i)		(o)
Ending balance	$3,000			(j)		(p)
Balance Sheet						
Total assets		(d)	$21,000			(q)
Liabilities	1,600		$ 5,000			(r)
Owner's Equity		(e)		(k)	380	
Total liabilities and owner's equity		(f)		(l)	$580	

Chapter 1, E 14.

Ridge Company
Income Statement
For the Year Ended June 30, 20x5

Revenues

Expenses

Net income

Ridge Company
Statement of Owner's Equity
For the Year Ended June 30, 20x5

Sy Ridge, Capital, June 30, 20x5

Ridge Company
Balance Sheet
June 30, 20x5

Assets		Liabilities	
		Owner's Equity	
Total assets		Total liabilities and owner's equity	

Chapter 1, E 15.

Waters Company
Statement of Cash Flows
For the Year Ended December 31, 20x4

Cash flows from operating activities		
Cash flows from investing activities		
Cash flows from financing activities		
Net increase (decrease) in cash		
Cash at beginning of year		
Cash at end of year		

Chapter 1, E 16.

AICPA:	
SEC:	
GAAP:	
FASB:	
IRS:	
GASB:	
IASB:	
IMA:	
CPA:	

Chapter 1, P 1.

1. Accounts arranged in equation form
2. Effects of transactions shown

		Assets					=	Liabilities	+	Owner's Equity	
		Cash	Accounts Receivable	Computer Supplies	Equipment	Systems Library		Accounts Payable		John Unger, Capital	Type of OE Transaction
a.	+	$18,000				+ $1,840				+ $19,840	Owner's Investment
b.	−	720				—				− 720	Rent Expense
bal.		$17,280				$1,840				$19,120	
c.											
bal.											
d.											
bal.											
e.											
bal.											
f.											
bal.											
g.											
bal.											
h.											
bal.											
i.											
bal.											
j.											
bal.											

Chapter 1, P 1. (Continued)

3. Cash flow effects discussed

Chapter 1, P 2.

1. Accounts arranged in equation form
2. Effects of transactions shown

	Assets				=	Liabilities	+	Owner's Equity	
	Cash	Accounts Receivable	Trucks	Equipment		Accounts Payable		Oscar Melendez, Capital	Type of OE Transaction
a.	+ $132,000							+ $132,000	Owner's Investment
b.									
bal.									
c.									
bal.									
d.									
bal.									
e.									
bal.									
f.									
bal.									
g.									
bal.									
h.									
bal.									
i.									
bal.									

Chapter 1, P 3.
1. Accounts arranged in equation form
2. Beginning balances entered
3. Effects of transactions shown

	Assets				=	Liabilities	+	Owner's Equity	
	Cash	Accounts Receivable	Office Supplies	Office Equipment		Accounts Payable		Sol Lindberg, Capital	Type of OE Transaction
bal.	$2,930	$1,400	$270	$4,200		$1,900		$6,900	
a.									
bal.									
b.									
bal.									
c.									
bal.									
d.									
bal.									
e.									
bal.									
f.									
bal.									
g.									
bal.									
h.									
bal.									
i.									
bal.									
j.									
bal.									
k.									
bal.									

Chapter 1, P 4.

1. Financial statements prepared

Moon Valley Riding Club
Income Statement
For the Month Ended September 30, 20xx

Revenues			
Expenses			
Net income			

Moon Valley Riding Club
Statement of Owner's Equity
For the Month Ended September 30, 20xx

Sheri Alexander, Capital, September 30, 20xx			

Moon Valley Riding Club
Balance Sheet
September 30, 20xx

Assets		Liabilities	
		Owner's Equity	
		Sheri Alexander, Capital	
Total assets		Total liabilities and owner's equity	

Chapter 1, P 4. (Continued)

2. Links among the financial statements identified

3. Statements associated with goals:

Chapter 1, P 5.

1. Accounts arranged in equation form
2. Effects of transactions shown

	Assets			=	Liabilities	+	Owner's Equity	
	Cash	Accounts Receivable	Supplies	Copier		Accounts Payable		M. Lomax, Capital	Type of OE Transaction
a.	+ $10,000							+ $10,000	Owner's Investment
b.									
bal.									
c.									
bal.									
d.									
bal.									
e.									
bal.									
f.									
bal.									
g.									
bal.									
h.									
bal.									
i.									
bal.									
j.									
bal.									
k.									
bal.									
l.									
bal.									

Chapter 1, P 5. (Continued)

3. Financial statements prepared

Arrow Copying Service
Income Statement
For the Month Ended August 31, 20xx

Revenues		
Expenses		
Net income		

Arrow Copying Service
Statement of Owner's Equity
For the Month Ended August 31, 20xx

M. Lomax, Capital, August 31, 20xx		

Arrow Copying Service
Balance Sheet
August 31, 20xx

Assets		Liabilities	
		Owner's Equity	
Total assets		Total liabilities and owner's equity	

Chapter 1, P 5. (Continued)

Arrow Copying Service
Statement of Cash Flows
For the Month Ended August 31, 20xx

Cash flows from operating activities		
Cash flows from investing activities		
Cash flows from financing activities		
Net increase (decrease) in cash		
Cash at beginning of month		
Cash at end of month		

Chapter 1, P 6.

1. Accounts arranged in equation form
2. Effects of transactions shown

	Assets			=	Liabilities	+	Owner's Equity	
	Cash	Accounts Receivable	Framing Supplies	Store Equipment		Accounts Payable		Rosa Partridge, Capital	Type of OE Transaction
a.									
b.									
bal.									
c.									
bal.									
d.									
bal.									
e.									
bal.									
f.									
bal.									
g.									
bal.									
h.									
bal.									
i.									
bal.									
j.									
bal.									

Chapter 1, P 6. (Continued)

3. Cash flow effects discussed

Chapter 1, P 7.

1. **Financial statements prepared**

Revenues		
Expenses		
Net income		

J. Ellis, Capital, March 31, 20xx

Assets		Liabilities	
		Owner's Equity	
Total assets		**Total liabilities and owner's equity**	

Chapter 1, P 7. (Continued)

2. Links among the financial statements identified

3. Statements associated with goals

Chapter 1, P 8.
1. Accounts arranged in equation form
2. Effects of transactions shown

	Assets			=	Liabilities	+	Owner's Equity
a.							
b.							
bal.							
c.							
bal.							
d.							
bal.							
e.							
bal.							
f.							
bal.							
g.							
bal.							
h.							
bal.							
i.							
bal.							
j.							
bal.							
k.							
bal.							
l.							
bal.							

Chapter 1, P 8. (Continued)

3. Financial statements prepared

Revenues		
Expenses		
Net income		

Madeline Curry, Capital, April 30, 20xx		

Assets		Liabilities	
		Owner's Equity	
Total assets		**Total liabilities and owner's equity**	

Chapter 1, P 8. (Continued)

Cash flows from operating activities		
Cash flows from investing activities		
Cash flows from financing activities		
Net increase (decrease) in cash		
Cash at beginning of month		
Cash at end of month		

Chapter 1, SD 1.

The three basic activities J.C. Penney will engage in to achieve its goals are:

Management role and functions:

Chapter 1, SD 2.

Individual or Group	Reason
1. Management	
2. Stockholders	
3. Creditors	
4. Potential stockholders	
5. Internal Revenue Service	
6. Securities and Exchange Commission	
7. Teamsters' union	
8. Consumers' group	
9. Economic adviser	

Importance of independent auditors' report

Chapter 1, SD 3.

Chapter 1, SD 4.

1.

2.

3.

4.

5.

6.

Chapter 1, SD 6.

1. Balance sheets prepared

	Henderson Lawn Care Company Balance Sheet June 1, 20xx		
Assets		Liabilities	
Cash			
		Owner's Equity	
Total assets		Total liabilities and owner's equity	

	Henderson Lawn Care Company Balance Sheet August 31, 20xx		
Assets		Liabilities	
		Owner's Equity	
Total assets		Total liabilities and owner's equity	

Chapter 1, SD 6. (Continued)

2. Memorandum prepared

Memorandum	
Date:	
To:	
From:	
Re:	

Chapter 1, FRA 1.

Some bodies that influence GAAP are as follows:

Chapter 1, FRA 2.

Chapter 1, FRA 3.

1.

2.

Chapter 1, FRA 4.

Chapter 1, FRA 5.

1. The names Toys "R" Us gives its four basic financial statements are as follows:

2. The accounting equation for Toys "R" Us for February 1, 2003, is as follows:

Assets	=	Liabilities	+	Stockholders' Equity
	=		+	

3. Total revenues of Toys "R" Us for 2002 were

4.

5.

6.

Chapter 1, FRA 6.

1.

2.

3.

4.

Chapter 1, FRA 8.

(in millions)	Microsoft (June 30, 2002)	Intel (December 28, 2002)
Total assets		
Revenues		
Net income		
Which company is larger?		
Which company is more profitable?		

Chapter 2, SE 1.

Jan.	10	
Feb.	15	
Mar.	1	

Chapter 2, SE 2.

Chapter 2, SE 3.

a.		e.	
b.		f.	
c.		g.	
d.		h.	

Chapter 2, SE 4.

a.		e.	
b.		f.	
c.		g.	
d.		h.	

Chapter 2, SE 5.

May	2	
	5	
	7	
	19	
	22	
	25	
	31	

Chapter 2, SE 6.

Cash		Accounts Receivable	

Supplies		Office Equipment	

Accounts Payable		Unearned Programming Service Revenue	

Deric Norman, Capital		Programming Service Revenue	

Rent Expense			

Chapter 2, SE 7.

Norman's Programming Service
Trial Balance
May 31, 20x5

Chapter 2, SE 8.

Duncan Boating Service
Trial Balance
January 31, 20x5

Chapter 2, SE 9.

General Journal

Date		Description	Post. Ref.	Debit	Credit
20xx					
Sept.	6				
	16				

Chapter 2, SE 10.

Cash — Account No. _____

Date	Item	Post. Ref.	Debit	Credit	Balance Debit	Balance Credit
20xx						

Accounts Receivable — Account No. _____

Date	Item	Post. Ref.	Debit	Credit	Balance Debit	Balance Credit
20xx						

Service Revenue — Account No. _____

Date	Item	Post. Ref.	Debit	Credit	Balance Debit	Balance Credit
20xx						

Chapter 2, E 1.

Feb.	17	
Mar.	7	
Apr.	28	
May	19	
June	27	

Chapter 2, E 2.

1. Purchases recognized on date shipped

Order	Date Shipped		Date Received	Amount
b	May	8		
			Total May purchases	

2. Purchases recognized on date received

Order	Date Shipped	Date Received	Amount
		Total May purchases	

Chapter 2, E 3.

Item	Type of Account						Normal Balance (increases balance)	
	Asset	Liability	Owner's Equity				Debit	Credit
			Owner's Capital	Owner's Withdrawals	Revenue	Expense		
a.	x						x	
b.								
c.								
d.								
e.								
f.								
g.								
h.								
i.								
j.								
k.								
l.								
m.								
n.								
o.								
p.								
q.								
r.								
s.								
t.								
u.								
v.								

Chapter 2, E 4.

a.

b.

c.

d.

e.

f.

g.

Chapter 2, E 5.

Cash		Repair Supplies		Repair Equipment	
a. 4,300				a. 1,600	

Accounts Payable		Jessie Sturchio, Capital		Jessie Sturchio, Withdrawals	
			a. 5,900		

Repair Fees Earned		Salaries Expense		Rent Expense	

Chapter 2, E 6.

Porcelain Cup Repair Service		
Trial Balance		
June 30, 20xx		

Chapter 2, E 7.

a.	
b.	
c.	
d.	
e.	
f.	
g.	
h.	

Chapter 2, E 8.

Chapter 2, E 9.

a.

b.

c.

d.

Chapter 2, E 10.

Fradin Services
Trial Balance
September 30, 20xx

Chapter 2, E 11.

Chapter 2, E 12.			
a.	Merchandise Inventory	1,600	
	Accounts Payable		1,600
	Purchased merchandise inventory		
	on account		

Chapter 2, E 13.

General Journal

Date	Description	Post. Ref.	Debit	Credit
20xx Dec.				

General Ledger

Cash — Account No. _____

Date	Item	Post. Ref.	Debit	Credit	Balance Debit	Balance Credit
20xx Dec. 13	Balance				8,000	

Equipment — Account No. _____

Date	Item	Post. Ref.	Debit	Credit	Balance Debit	Balance Credit
20xx						

Accounts Payable — Account No. _____

Date	Item	Post. Ref.	Debit	Credit	Balance Debit	Balance Credit
20xx						

Chapter 2, P 1.

		Debit	Credit
a.			
b.			
c.			
d.			
e.			
f.			
g.			
h.			
i.			
j.			
k.			
l.			
m.			
n.			

Chapter 2, P 2.

1. T accounts set up
2. Transactions recorded in the accounts

Cash	Accounts Receivable	Software

Furniture	Microcomputers	Accounts Payable

Kyle Piu, Capital	Kyle Piu, Withdrawals	Tuition Revenue

Wages Expense	Utilities Expense	Rent Expense

Advertising Expense		

Chapter 2, P 2. (Continued)

3. **Trial balance prepared**

Computer Skills Training Center
Trial Balance

4. **Cash flow effects discussed**

Chapter 2, P 3.

1. Transactions entered in the general journal

General Journal

Page ___

Date		Description	Post. Ref.	Debit	Credit
20xx					
Oct.	1	Cash	111	6,000	
		Dee Strong, Capital	311		6,000
		Invested in business			

Chapter 2, P 3. (Continued)

Date	Description	Post. Ref.	Debit	Credit
20xx				

Chapter 2, P 3. (Continued)

2. Ledger accounts set up and journal entries posted

General Ledger

Cash — Account No. _____

Date	Item	Post. Ref.	Debit	Credit	Balance Debit	Balance Credit
20xx Oct.						

Accounts Receivable — Account No. _____

Date	Item	Post. Ref.	Debit	Credit	Balance Debit	Balance Credit
20xx						

Cleaning Supplies — Account No. _____

Date	Item	Post. Ref.	Debit	Credit	Balance Debit	Balance Credit
20xx						

Chapter 2, P 3. (Continued)

Prepaid Lease — Account No. _____

Date	Item	Post. Ref.	Debit	Credit	Balance Debit	Balance Credit
20xx						

Cleaning Equipment — Account No. _____

Date	Item	Post. Ref.	Debit	Credit	Balance Debit	Balance Credit
20xx						

Accounts Payable — Account No. _____

Date	Item	Post. Ref.	Debit	Credit	Balance Debit	Balance Credit
20xx						

Dee Strong, Capital — Account No. _____

Date	Item	Post. Ref.	Debit	Credit	Balance Debit	Balance Credit
20xx						

Dee Strong, Withdrawals — Account No. _____

Date	Item	Post. Ref.	Debit	Credit	Balance Debit	Balance Credit
20xx						

Chapter 2, P 3. (Continued)

Cleaning Revenues   Account No. _____

Date	Item	Post. Ref.	Debit	Credit	Balance Debit	Credit
20xx						

Repair Expense   Account No. _____

Date	Item	Post. Ref.	Debit	Credit	Balance Debit	Credit
20xx						

3. Trial balance prepared

Strong's Office-Cleaning Service
Trial Balance
October 31, 20xx

Chapter 2, P 3. (Continued)

4. Accounting issues discussed

Chapter 2, P 4.

1. Transactions entered in journal form

20xx				
June	3	Equipment	2,460	
		Cash	14,200	
		Ben Aronson, Capital		16,660
		Invested equipment and cash in business		

Chapter 2, P 4. (Continued)

20xx

Chapter 2, P. 4. (Continued)

2. T accounts set up and entries posted from the journal

Cash	Accounts Receivable	Supplies
6/3		
Bal.		

Prepaid Insurance	Equipment	Truck

Notes Payable	Accounts Payable	Ben Aronson, Capital

Ben Aronson, Withdrawals	Painting Fees Earned	Wages Expense

Telephone Expense	Repair Expense	

Chapter 2, P 4. (Continued)

3. Trial balance prepared

Aronson Painting Service
Trial Balance
June 30, 20xx

Chapter 2, P 4. (Continued)

4. Recognition and classification discussed

Chapter 2, P 5.

1. Transactions entered in the general journal

General Journal   Page ___

Date		Description	Post. Ref.	Debit	Credit
20xx					
Sept.	3	Rent Expense	511	540	
		Cash	111		540
		Paid September rent			

Chapter 2, P 5. (Continued)

Date	Description	Post. Ref.	Debit	Credit
20xx				

Chapter 2, P 5. (Continued)

2. Ledger accounts set up
3. Amounts from August 31 trial balance entered
4. Entries from journal posted to ledger accounts

General Ledger

Cash   Account No. _____

Date	Item	Post. Ref.	Debit	Credit	Balance Debit	Balance Credit
20xx						
Aug. 31	Balance					

Accounts Receivable   Account No. _____

Date	Item	Post. Ref.	Debit	Credit	Balance Debit	Balance Credit
20xx						

Supplies   Account No. _____

Date	Item	Post. Ref.	Debit	Credit	Balance Debit	Balance Credit
20xx						

Chapter 2, P 5. (Continued)

Prepaid Insurance   Account No. _____

Date	Item	Post. Ref.	Debit	Credit	Balance Debit	Balance Credit
20xx						

Equipment   Account No. _____

Date	Item	Post. Ref.	Debit	Credit	Balance Debit	Balance Credit
20xx						

Buses   Account No. _____

Date	Item	Post. Ref.	Debit	Credit	Balance Debit	Balance Credit
20xx						

Notes Payable   Account No. _____

Date	Item	Post. Ref.	Debit	Credit	Balance Debit	Balance Credit
20xx						

Accounts Payable   Account No. _____

Date	Item	Post. Ref.	Debit	Credit	Balance Debit	Balance Credit
20xx						

Chapter 2, P 5. (Continued)

Lisa Corvelli, Capital   Account No. _____

Date	Item	Post. Ref.	Debit	Credit	Balance Debit	Balance Credit
20xx						

Lisa Corvelli, Withdrawals   Account No. _____

Date	Item	Post. Ref.	Debit	Credit	Balance Debit	Balance Credit
20xx						

Service Revenue   Account No. _____

Date	Item	Post. Ref.	Debit	Credit	Balance Debit	Balance Credit
20xx						

Rent Expense   Account No. _____

Date	Item	Post. Ref.	Debit	Credit	Balance Debit	Balance Credit
20xx						

Gasoline Expense   Account No. _____

Date	Item	Post. Ref.	Debit	Credit	Balance Debit	Balance Credit
20xx						

Chapter 2, P 5. (Continued)

Wages Expense   Account No. _____

Date	Item	Post. Ref.	Debit	Credit	Balance Debit	Balance Credit
20xx						

Utilities Expense   Account No. _____

Date	Item	Post. Ref.	Debit	Credit	Balance Debit	Balance Credit
20xx						

5. Trial balance prepared

6. Trial balance discussed

Chapter 2, P 6.

		Debit	Credit
a.			
b.			
c.			
d.			
e.			
f.			
g.			
h.			
i.			
j.			
k.			
l.			
m.			
n.			

Chapter 2, P 7.

1. Transactions entered in journal form

20xx				
May	3	Cash	14,400	
		Marcus Stahl, Capital		14,400
		Owner's investment		

Chapter 2, P 7. (Continued)

20xx				

Chapter 2, P 7. (Continued)

2. T accounts set up and entries posted from the journal.

Cash	Accounts Receivable	Supplies

Bal.

Shed	Bicycles	Accounts Payable

Marcus Stahl, Capital	Marcus Stahl, Withdrawals	Rental Revenue

Wages Expense	Maintenance Expense	Repair Expense

Concession Fee Expense		

Chapter 2, P 7. (Continued)

3. Trial balance prepared

4. Recognition and classification discussed

Chapter 2, P 8.

1. Transactions entered in the general journal

General Journal   Page ___

Date		Description	Post. Ref.	Debit	Credit
20xx					
May	3	Rent Expense	512	1,300	
		Cash	111		1,300
		Paid May rent			

Chapter 2, P 8. (Continued)

General Journal

Page ___

Date	Description	Post. Ref.	Debit	Credit
20xx				

Chapter 2, P 8. (Continued)

2. **Ledger accounts set up**
3. **Amounts from April 30 trial balance entered**
4. **Entries from journal posted to ledger accounts**

General Ledger

Cash   Account No. _____

Date		Item	Post. Ref.	Debit	Credit	Balance Debit	Balance Credit
20xx							
Apr.	30	Balance				20,400	

Accounts Receivable   Account No. _____

Date	Item	Post. Ref.	Debit	Credit	Balance Debit	Balance Credit
20xx						

Supplies   Account No. _____

Date	Item	Post. Ref.	Debit	Credit	Balance Debit	Balance Credit
20xx						

Chapter 2, P 8. (Continued)

Office Equipment   Account No. _____

Date	Item	Post. Ref.	Debit	Credit	Balance Debit	Balance Credit
20xx						

Accounts Payable   Account No. _____

Date	Item	Post. Ref.	Debit	Credit	Balance Debit	Balance Credit
20xx						

Samantha Young, Capital   Account No. _____

Date	Item	Post. Ref.	Debit	Credit	Balance Debit	Balance Credit
20xx						

Samantha Young, Withdrawals   Account No. _____

Date	Item	Post. Ref.	Debit	Credit	Balance Debit	Balance Credit
20xx						

Marketing Fees   Account No. _____

Date	Item	Post. Ref.	Debit	Credit	Balance Debit	Balance Credit
20xx						

Chapter 2, P 8. (Continued)

Salaries Expense — Account No. _____

Date	Item	Post. Ref.	Debit	Credit	Balance Debit	Balance Credit
20xx						

Rent Expense — Account No. _____

Date	Item	Post. Ref.	Debit	Credit	Balance Debit	Balance Credit
20xx						

Utilities Expense — Account No. _____

Date	Item	Post. Ref.	Debit	Credit	Balance Debit	Balance Credit
20xx						

Telephone Expense — Account No. _____

Date	Item	Post. Ref.	Debit	Credit	Balance Debit	Balance Credit
20xx						

Advertising Expense — Account No. _____

Date	Item	Post. Ref.	Debit	Credit	Balance Debit	Balance Credit
20xx						

Chapter 2, P 8. (Continued)

5. Trial balance prepared

6. Trial balance discussed

Chapter 2, SD 1.

Memorandum

Date:
To:
From:
Re:

Chapter 2, SD 2.

a.

b.

c.

Chapter 2, SD 3.

Chapter 2, SD 5.

1. June transactions recorded in journal form

Cash	23,000	
Ben Obi, Capital		23,000
Invested in business		

Chapter 2, SD 5. (Continued)

2. Entries set up in T accounts

Cash	Accounts Receivable	Prepaid Rent

Bal.

Truck	Office Equipment	Repair Tools

Accounts Payable	Unearned Revenue	Loan Payable

Truck Loan Payable	Ben Obi, Capital	Repair Revenue

Wages Expense	Utilities Expense	Interest Expense

Legal Expense		

Chapter 2, SD 5. (Continued)

3. Trial balance prepared

<table>
<tr><td colspan="3" align="center">**Obi Repairs Company**
Trial Balance
June 30, 20xx</td></tr>
<tr><td></td><td></td><td></td></tr>
</table>

4. Information in trial balance evaluated

Chapter 2, SD 5. (Continued)

Chapter 2, FRA 1.

1. Accounts classified

Cash and Due from Banks		
Loans to Customers		
Securities available for sale		
Deposits by Customers		

2. Transactions recorded in journal form

a.			
b.			
c.			

Chapter 2, FRA 2.

(Numbers are in millions of yen)

Chapter 2, FRA 3.

(Numbers are in millions)

Cash and Cash Equivalents

Bal.

Accounts and Other Receivables

Prepaid Expenses and Other Current Assets

Accounts Payable

Income Taxes Payable

Chapter 2, FRA 4.

1.

2.

3.

Differences discussed:

Chapter 3, SE 1.

1.
2.
3.
4.

Chapter 3, SE 2.

Dec.	31			

Chapter 3, SE 3.

Dec.	31			

Chapter 3, SE 4.

Balance Sheet Presentation:

Chapter 3, SE 5.

Chapter 3, SE 6.

Aug.	31			

Chapter 3, SE 7.

<table>
<tr><td colspan="3">Hailston Company
Income Statement
For the Month Ended December 31, 20x3</td></tr>
<tr><td>Revenues</td><td></td><td></td></tr>
<tr><td>Expenses</td><td></td><td></td></tr>
<tr><td></td><td></td><td></td></tr>
<tr><td></td><td></td><td></td></tr>
<tr><td></td><td></td><td></td></tr>
<tr><td></td><td></td><td></td></tr>
<tr><td>Net income</td><td></td><td></td></tr>
</table>

Chapter 3, SE 8.

Chapter 3, SE 9.

Chapter 3, SE 10.

Chapter 3, E 1.

1.		4.	
2.		5.	
3.		6.	

Chapter 3, E 2.

a.	
b.	
c.	
d.	

Chapter 3, E 3.

20x3			

Chapter 3, E 4.

1.

2.

Chapter 3, E 5.

1. Fill in the missing amounts:

	a	b	c	d
Supplies on hand, October 1	$396	$ 651	$294	
+ Supplies purchased during the month	78		261	2,892
= Total supplies available				
− Supplies consumed during the month	291	1,458		2,448
= Supplies on hand, October 31		$ 654	$ 84	$1,782

2. Adjusting entry for Column a

Oct. 31

Chapter 3, E 6.

1. July 31

2.

Chapter 3, E 7.

1. Royalty expense and royalty income calculated

2. Adjusting entries recorded

In Celestial Systems Company's records:

20x3				
Dec.	31			

In Swan Company's records:

20x3				
Dec.	31			

Chapter 3, E 8.

1.	Office Supplies Expense		
	Office Supplies		
	To record supplies consumed during		
	period		
2.			
3.			
4.			
5.			
6.			

Chapter 3, E 9.

1. Entries recorded

Apr.	1			
Dec.	31			

2.

Chapter 3, E 10.

Revenues		
Expenses		
Total expenses		
Net income		

Chapter 3, E 10. (Continued)

Assets

Total assets

Liabilities

Owner's Equity

Total liabilities and owner's equity

Chapter 3, E 11.

Insurance Expense:
- Beginning Prepaid Insurance
- Cash disbursements for insurance
- Subtotal
- Less ending Prepaid Insurance
- Insurance Expense

Wages Expense:

Fees Earned:

Chapter 3, E 12.

Chapter 3, E 13.

1. Cash paid for rent during the year:
   Ending balance
   Rent Expense
   Potential cash paid for rent
   Less beginning balance
   Cash paid during the year

2. Cash paid for interest during the year:

3. Cash paid for salaries during the year:

Chapter 3, P 1.

	Balance Sheet Account	Amount of Adjustment (+ or –)	Balance after Adjustment	Income Statement Account	Amount of Adjustment (+ or –)	Balance after Adjustment
a.	Prepaid Insurance	– $2,720	$ 680	Insurance Expense	+ $2,720	$ 2,720
b.						
c.						
d.						
e.						
f.						

Chapter 3, P 2.

1. Adjusting entries prepared

a.	June	30	Interest Expense	12,000	
			Interest Payable		12,000
			To record accrued interest on mortgage		

Chapter 3, P 2. (Continued)

2. Revenue recognition discussed

Chapter 3, P 3.

1. T accounts set up and balances entered
2. Adjusting entries posted to the accounts

Cash	Accounts Receivable	Office Supplies
Bal. 25,572		

Prepaid Rent	Office Equipment	Accumulated Depreciation, Office Equipment

Accounts Payable	Notes Payable	Interest Payable

Salaries Payable	Unearned Service Revenue	James Georgios, Capital

James Georgios, Withdrawals	Service Revenue	Salaries Expense

Utilities Expense	Rent Expense	Office Supplies Expense

Depreciation Expense, Office Equipment	Interest Expense	

Chapter 3, P 3. (Continued)

3. Adjusted trial balance prepared

Omega Advisory Company
Adjusted Trial Balance
March 31, 20x4

Chapter 3, P 4.

1. Adjusting entries recorded in the general journal

General Journal Page ___

Date		Description	Post. Ref.	Debit	Credit
20x4					
Oct.	31	Supplies Expense	513	78	
		Supplies	115		78
		To record supplies used			

Chapter 3, P 4. (Continued)

2. Ledger accounts opened and balances recorded
3. Adjusting entries posted from the general journal

Cash
Account No. _____

Date	Item	Post. Ref.	Debit	Credit	Balance Debit	Balance Credit
20x4						

Accounts Receivable
Account No. _____

Date	Item	Post. Ref.	Debit	Credit	Balance Debit	Balance Credit
20x4						

Supplies
Account No. _____

Date	Item	Post. Ref.	Debit	Credit	Balance Debit	Balance Credit
20x4						

Prepaid Rent
Account No. _____

Date	Item	Post. Ref.	Debit	Credit	Balance Debit	Balance Credit
20x4						

Prepaid Insurance
Account No. _____

Date	Item	Post. Ref.	Debit	Credit	Balance Debit	Balance Credit
20x4						

Chapter 3, P 4. (Continued)

Equipment   Account No. _____

Date	Item	Post. Ref.	Debit	Credit	Balance Debit	Balance Credit
20x4						

Accumulated Depreciation, Equipment   Account No. _____

Date	Item	Post. Ref.	Debit	Credit	Balance Debit	Balance Credit
20x4						

Accounts Payable   Account No. _____

Date	Item	Post. Ref.	Debit	Credit	Balance Debit	Balance Credit
20x4						

Wages Payable   Account No. _____

Date	Item	Post. Ref.	Debit	Credit	Balance Debit	Balance Credit
20x4						

Unearned Dance Fees   Account No. _____

Date	Item	Post. Ref.	Debit	Credit	Balance Debit	Balance Credit
20x4						

Margrit Berger, Capital   Account No. _____

Date	Item	Post. Ref.	Debit	Credit	Balance Debit	Balance Credit
20x4						

Chapter 3, P 4. (Continued)

Margrit Berger, Withdrawals   Account No. _____

Date	Item	Post. Ref.	Debit	Credit	Balance Debit	Balance Credit
20x4						

Dance Fees   Account No. _____

Date	Item	Post. Ref.	Debit	Credit	Balance Debit	Balance Credit
20x4						

Wages Expense   Account No. _____

Date	Item	Post. Ref.	Debit	Credit	Balance Debit	Balance Credit
20x4						

Rent Expense   Account No. _____

Date	Item	Post. Ref.	Debit	Credit	Balance Debit	Balance Credit
20x4						

Supplies Expense   Account No. _____

Date	Item	Post. Ref.	Debit	Credit	Balance Debit	Balance Credit
20x4						

Insurance Expense   Account No. _____

Date	Item	Post. Ref.	Debit	Credit	Balance Debit	Balance Credit
20x4						

Chapter 3, P 4. (Continued)

Utilities Expense   Account No. _____

Date	Item	Post. Ref.	Debit	Credit	Balance Debit	Balance Credit
20x4						

Depreciation Expense, Equipment   Account No. _____

Date	Item	Post. Ref.	Debit	Credit	Balance Debit	Balance Credit
20x4						

Chapter 3, P 4. (Continued)

4. Adjusted trial balance, income statement, statement of owner's equity, and balance sheet prepared

<table>
<tr><td colspan="3" align="center">Broadway Dance Studio
Adjusted Trial Balance
October 31, 20x4</td></tr>
<tr><td></td><td></td><td></td></tr>
</table>

Chapter 3, P 4. (Continued)

Broadway Dance Studio
Income Statement
For the Year Ended October 31, 20x4

Revenues

Expenses

Net income

Broadway Dance Studio
Statement of Owner's Equity
For the Year Ended October 31, 20x4

Chapter 3, P 4. (Continued)

Broadway Dance Studio
Balance Sheet
October 31, 20x4

Assets

Liabilities

Owner's Equity

Total liabilities and owner's equity

Chapter 3, P 5.

1. T accounts set up and balances entered
2. Adjusting entries posted to the accounts

Cash	Accounts Receivable	Prepaid Insurance
Bal. 2,268		

Office Supplies	Office Equipment	Accumulated Depreciation, Office Equipment

Copier	Accumulated Depreciation, Copier	Accounts Payable

Unearned Service Revenue	Bonnie Vitali, Capital	Bonnie Vitali, Withdrawals

Service Revenue	Office Salaries Expense	Advertising Expense

Rent Expense	Telephone Expense	Insurance Expense

Office Supplies Expense	Depreciation Expense, Office Equipment	Depreciation Expense, Copier

Chapter 3, P 5. (Continued)

3. Adjusted trial balance, income statement, statement of owner's equity, and balance sheet prepared

Adjusted Trial Balance

Chapter 3, P 5. (Continued)

Income Statement

Revenues

Expenses

Net income

Statement of Owner's Equity

Chapter 3, P 5. (Continued)

Balance Sheet

Assets

Total assets

Liabilities

Owner's Equity

Total liabilities and owner's equity

Chapter 3, P 6.

Balance Sheet Account	Amount of Adjustment (+ or −)	Balance after Adjustment	Income Statement Account	Amount of Adjustment (+ or −)	Balance after Adjustment
a. Office Supplies	− $770	$133	Office Supplies Expense	+ $770	$770

Chapter 3, P 7.

1. Adjusting entries prepared

a.	May	31	Supplies Expense		10,606	
			Supplies			10,606
			To record supplies used			

Chapter 3, P 7. (Continued)

2. Revenue recognition discussed

Chapter 3, P 8.

1. T accounts set up and balances entered
2. Adjusting entries posted to the accounts

Cash	Accounts Receivable	Office Supplies
Bal. 16,500		

Prepaid Rent	Office Equipment	Accumulated Depreciation, Office Equipment

Accounts Payable	Notes Payable	Interest Payable

Salaries Payable	Unearned Service Revenue	Stephanie Wu, Capital

Stephanie Wu, Withdrawals	Service Revenue	Salaries Expense

Rent Expense	Utilities Expense	Office Supplies Expense

Depreciation Expense, Office Equipment	Interest Expense	

Chapter 3, P 8. (Continued)

3. Adjusted trial balance prepared

Chapter 3, SD 1.

Chapter 3, SD 2.

Chapter 3, SD 3.

Chapter 3, SD 5.

1. Adjusting entries prepared

a.	Printing Supplies Expense	18,000	
	Printing Supplies		18,000
	Recording of supplies used		

Chapter 3, SD 5. (Continued)

2. Financial statement amounts recast

	Before	Adjustments				After
Revenues						
Expenses		(a)				
Net income						
Total assets						
Liabilities						
Owner's equity						
Total liabilities and owner's equity						

3. Results discussed

Chapter 3, FRA 1.

1. Film and television costs defined

2. T accounts set up to record the amount spent

Cash		Film and Television Costs	

3. T accounts set up to record the amount expensed

Adjusting Entry

Film and Television Costs (amortization)		Film and Television Costs	

4. Matching rule discussed

Chapter 3, FRA 2.

1. Current liabilities identified (in thousands)

The following current liabilities definitely would have arisen from adjusting entries:

Total	

Part of the following current liabilities probably arose from adjusting entries:

Total	

The following accounts probably did not arise from adjusting entries:

Total	

2. Effects of adjustments explained

Chapter 3, FRA 3.

Chapter 3, FRA 4.

Chapter 3, FRA 5.

1.

2. The ratio of depreciation and amortization to net sales for each company for the most recent year is as follows:

(in millions)	Walgreens	Toys "R" Us
Depreciation and Amortization Expense		
Net Sales		
Ratio of Depreciation and Amortization to Net Sales		

These percentages are small because:

3.

Chapter 4, SE 1.

Chapter 4, SE 2.

Dec.	31			

Chapter 4, SE 3.

Dec.	31			

Chapter 4, SE 4.

Dec.	31			

Chapter 4, SE 5.

Dec.	31			

Chapter 4, SE 6.

H. Blake, Capital	H. Blake, Withdrawals

Income Summary	Patient Services Revenues

Laboratory Fees Revenues	Rent Expense

Wages Expense	Other Expenses

Chapter 4, SE 7.

Chapter 4, SE 8.

Salaries Payable	Salaries Expense

Chapter 4, SE 9.

Dec.	31			

Chapter 4, E 1.

Dec.	31			

Chapter 4, E 2.

1. **Appropriateness of reversing entry explained**

2. **Reversing entry prepared**

20xx				
Oct.	1			

3. **Entry for payment of wages**

20xx				
Oct.	5			

Chapter 4, E 3.

Chapter 4, E 4.

1. Trial balance amounts entered on the work sheet
2. Work sheet completed

For the Month Ended March 31, 20xx

Account Name	Trial Balance		Adjustments		Adjusted Trial Balance		Income Statement		Balance Sheet	
	Debit	Credit	Debit	Credit	Debit	Credit	Debit	Credit	Debit	Credit

Chapter 4, E 5.

Sariah's Clip Shop
Statement of Owner's Equity
For the Year Ended December 31, 20x4

Chapter 4, E 6.

1. Adjustments made

   (a)

2. Balance sheet prepared

Balance Sheet

Assets

Liabilities

Owner's Equity

Chapter 4, E 7.

1. Adjusting entries prepared

	20xx				
(a)	June	30	Insurance Expense	240	
			Prepaid Insurance		240
			Recorded expired insurance		

2. Appropriate reversing entry (entries) prepared

	20xx				

Chapter 4, E 8.

20xx				

Chapter 4, P 1.

1. T accounts opened and balances entered
2. Closing entries entered in T accounts

Susan Wilde, Capital

Susan Wilde, Withdrawals

Income Summary

Revenues from Court Fees

Revenues from Locker Fees

Wages Expense

Maintenance Expense

Advertising Expense

Utilities Expense

Supplies Expense

Chapter 4, P 1. (Continued)

	Depreciation Expense, Building		
	Depreciation Expense, Equipment		
	Property Taxes Expense		
	Miscellaneous Expense		

Chapter 4, P 1. (Continued)

3. Income statement, statement of owner's equity, and balance sheet prepared

Applewilde Tennis Club
Income Statement
For the Year Ended June 30, 20x5

Revenues

Expenses

Net income

Applewilde Tennis Club
Statement of Owner's Equity
For the Year Ended June 30, 20x5

Chapter 4, P 1. (Continued)

Applewilde Tennis Club
Balance Sheet
June 30, 20x5

Assets

Liabilities

Owner's Equity

Total liabilities and owner's equity

4. Reason for closing entries explained

Chapter 4, P 2.

1. Closing entries prepared

20x5				

Chapter 4, P 2. (Continued)

2. Income statement, statement of owner's equity, and balance sheet prepared

Revenues

Expenses

Net income

Chapter 4, P 2. (Continued)

Assets

Liabilities

Owner's Equity

3. Reversing entry prepared

20x5			

Chapter 4, P 3.

1. Journal entries for October prepared
3. Adjusting entries for October prepared
6. Closing entries for October prepared

General Journal

Page

Date	Description	Post. Ref.	Debit	Credit
20xx				
Oct. 1				

Chapter 4, P 3. (Continued)

General Journal

Date	Description	Post. Ref.	Debit	Credit
20xx				

Chapter 4, P 3. (Continued)

General Journal

Date	Description	Post. Ref.	Debit	Credit

Chapter 4, P 3. (Continued)

4. October adjusted trial balance prepared

Dauphinais Appliance Service
Adjusted Trial Balance
October 31, 20xx

Chapter 4, P 3. (Continued)

5. October income statement, statement of owner's equity, and balance sheet prepared

Dauphinais Appliance Service
Income Statement
For the Month Ended October 31, 20xx

Revenues

Expenses

Net income

Dauphinais Appliance Service
Statement of Owner's Equity
For the Month Ended October 31, 20xx

Chapter 4, P 3. (Continued)

Dauphinais Appliance Service
Balance Sheet
October 31, 20xx

Assets

Total assets

Liabilities

Owner's Equity

Total liabilities and owner's equity

7. October post-closing trial balance prepared

Dauphinais Appliance Service
Post-Closing Trial Balance
October 31, 20xx

Chapter 4, P 3. (Continued)

8. Journal entries for November prepared
9. Adjusting entries for November prepared
12. Closing entries for November prepared

General Journal

Page:

Date	Description	Post. Ref.	Debit	Credit
20xx				

Chapter 4, P 3. (Continued)

General Journal

Page

Date	Description	Post. Ref.	Debit	Credit

Chapter 4, P 3. (Continued)

General Journal

Date	Description	Post. Ref.	Debit	Credit

Chapter 4, P 3. (Continued)

2. Accounts opened and October entries posted
3. Adjusting entries for October posted
6. Closing entries for October posted
8. November entries posted
9. Adjusting entries for November posted
12. Closing entries for November posted

Cash — Account No. 111

Date		Item	Post. Ref.	Debit	Credit	Balance Debit	Balance Credit
20xx							
Oct.	1						
	1						
	1						
	2						
	8						
	15						
	21						
	31						
	31						
Nov.	1						
	1						
	15						
	20						
	23						
	30						
	30						

Prepaid Insurance — Account No. 117

Date		Item	Post. Ref.	Debit	Credit	Balance Debit	Balance Credit
20xx							
Oct.	1						
	31						
Nov.	30						

Chapter 4, P 3. (Continued)

Repair Supplies — Account No. 119

Date		Item	Post. Ref.	Debit	Credit	Balance Debit	Balance Credit
20xx							
Oct.	5						
	31						
Nov.	6						
	30						

Repair Equipment — Account No. 144

Date		Item	Post. Ref.	Debit	Credit	Balance Debit	Balance Credit
20xx							
Oct.	2						

Accumulated Depreciation, Repair Equipment — Account No. 145

Date		Item	Post. Ref.	Debit	Credit	Balance Debit	Balance Credit
20xx							
Oct.	31						
Nov.	30						

Accounts Payable — Account No. 212

Date		Item	Post. Ref.	Debit	Credit	Balance Debit	Balance Credit
20xx							
Oct.	2						
	5						
	21						
Nov.	1						
	6						
	23						

Chapter 4, P 3. (Continued)

J. Dauphinais, Capital — Account No. 311

Date		Item	Post. Ref.	Debit	Credit	Balance Debit	Balance Credit
20xx							
Oct.	1						
	31						
	31						
Nov.	30						
	30						

J. Dauphinais, Withdrawals — Account No. 312

Date		Item	Post. Ref.	Debit	Credit	Balance Debit	Balance Credit
20xx							
Oct.	31						
	31						
Nov.	30						
	30						

Income Summary — Account No. 313

Date		Item	Post. Ref.	Debit	Credit	Balance Debit	Balance Credit
20xx							
Oct.	31						
	31						
	31						
Nov.	30						
	30						
	30						

Chapter 4, P 3. (Continued)

Repair Revenue — Account No. 411

Date		Item	Post. Ref.	Debit	Credit	Balance Debit	Balance Credit
20xx							
Oct.	15						
	31						
	31						
Nov.	15						
	30						
	30						

Store Rent Expense — Account No. 511

Date		Item	Post. Ref.	Debit	Credit	Balance Debit	Balance Credit
20xx							
Oct.	1						
	31						
Nov.	1						
	30						

Advertising Expense — Account No. 512

Date		Item	Post. Ref.	Debit	Credit	Balance Debit	Balance Credit
20xx							
Oct.	8						
	31						
Nov.	20						
	30						

Chapter 4, P 3. (Continued)

Insurance Expense   Account No. 513

Date		Item	Post. Ref.	Debit	Credit	Balance Debit	Balance Credit
20xx							
Oct.	31						
	31						
Nov.	30						
	30						

Repair Supplies Expense   Account No. 514

Date		Item	Post. Ref.	Debit	Credit	Balance Debit	Balance Credit
20xx							
Oct.	31						
	31						
Nov.	30						
	30						

Depreciation Expense, Repair Equipment   Account No. 515

Date		Item	Post. Ref.	Debit	Credit	Balance Debit	Balance Credit
20xx							
Oct.	31						
	31						
Nov.	30						
	30						

Chapter 4, P 3. (Continued)

10. November adjusted trial balance prepared

Dauphinais Appliance Service
Adjusted Trial Balance
November 30, 20xx

Chapter 4, P 3. (Continued)

11. November income statement, statement of owner's equity, and balance sheet prepared

Dauphinais Appliance Service
Income Statement
For the Month Ended November 30, 20xx

Revenues

Expenses

Net income

Dauphinais Appliance Service
Statement of Owner's Equity
For the Month Ended November 30, 20xx

Chapter 4, P 3. (Continued)

Dauphinais Appliance Service
Balance Sheet
November 30, 20xx

Assets

Liabilities

Owner's Equity

13. November post-closing trial balance prepared

Dauphinais Appliance Service
Post-Closing Trial Balance
November 30, 20xx

Chapter 4, P 4.

1. Work sheet completed

Jacqueline Woo Executive Search Service
Work Sheet
For the Six Months Ended December 31, 20x4

Account Name	Trial Balance Debit	Trial Balance Credit	Adjustments Debit	Adjustments Credit	Adjusted Trial Balance Debit	Adjusted Trial Balance Credit	Income Statement Debit	Income Statement Credit	Balance Sheet Debit	Balance Sheet Credit
Cash	713									
Accounts Receivable	1,000									
Prepaid Rent	1,800			(a) 900						
Office Supplies	413									
Office Equipment	15,750									
Accumulated Depreciation, Office Equipment										
Accounts Payable		3,173								
Unearned Revenues		1,823								
Jacqueline Woo, Capital		10,000								
Jacqueline Woo, Withdrawals	5,200									
Search Revenue		20,140								
Utilities Expense	1,260									
Wages Expense	9,000									
	35,136	35,136								
Rent Expense										
Office Supplies Expense										
Depreciation Expense, Office Equipment										
Wages Payable										
Net Income										

Chapter 4, P. 4. (Continued)

2. Income statement, statement of owner's equity, and balance sheet prepared

Jacqueline Woo Executive Search Service
Income Statement
For the Six Months Ended December 31, 20x4

Revenues

Expenses

Net income

Jacqueline Woo Executive Search Service
Statement of Owner's Equity
For the Six Months Ended December 31, 20x4

Chapter 4, P 4. (Continued)

Jacqueline Woo Executive Search Service
Balance Sheet
December 31, 20x4

Assets

Liabilities

Owner's Equity

Chapter 4, P 4. (Continued)

3. Adjusting, closing, and reversing entries prepared

20x4

Chapter 4, P 4. (Continued)

20x4				

Chapter 4, P 4. (Continued)

4.

Chapter 4, P 5.

1. Work sheet completed

McIntire Express Delivery Company—Work Sheet—For the Year Ended August 31, 20x4

Account Name	Trial Balance Debit	Trial Balance Credit	Adjustments Debit	Adjustments Credit	Adjusted Trial Balance Debit	Adjusted Trial Balance Credit	Income Statement Debit	Income Statement Credit	Balance Sheet Debit	Balance Sheet Credit
Cash	5,036									
Accounts Receivable	14,657									
Prepaid Insurance	2,670									
Delivery Supplies	7,350									
Office Supplies	1,230									
Land	7,500									
Building	98,000									
Accumulated Depreciation, Building		26,700								
Trucks	51,900									
Accumulated Depreciation, Trucks		15,450								
Office Equipment	7,950									
Accumulated Depreciation, Office Equipment		5,400								
Accounts Payable		4,698								
Unearned Lockbox Fees		4,170								
Mortgage Payable		36,000								
Matt McIntire, Capital		64,365								
Matt McIntire, Withdrawals	15,000									
Delivery Services Revenue		141,735								
Lockbox Fees Earned		14,400								
Truck Drivers' Wages Expense	63,900									
Office Salaries Expense	22,200									
Gas, Oil, and Truck Repairs Expense	15,525									
	312,918	312,918								
Net Income										

Chapter 4, P 5. (Continued)

2. Income statement, statement of owner's equity, and balance sheet prepared

Revenues

Expenses

Net income

	McIntire Express Delivery Company Statement of Owner's Equity For the Year Ended August 31, 20x4		

(continued)

Chapter 4, P 5. (Continued)

Assets

Total assets

Liabilities

Owner's Equity

Chapter 4, P 5. (Continued)

3. Adjusting, closing, and reversing entries prepared

20x4

Chapter 4, P 5. (Continued)

20x4

Chapter 4, P 6.

1. T accounts opened and balances entered
2. Closing entries entered in T accounts

Tom Wells, Capital

Tom Wells, Withdrawals

Income Summary

Revenues

Wages Expense

Advertising Expense

Maintenance Expense

Supplies Expense

Insurance Expense

Depreciation Expense, Building

Chapter 4, P 6. (Continued)

	Depreciation Expense, Equipment		
	Utilities Expense		
	Miscellaneous Expense		
	Property Taxes Expense		

Chapter 4, P 6. (Continued)

3. Income statement, statement of owner's equity, and balance sheet prepared

Hartford Go-Cart Lanes
Income Statement
For the Year Ended December 31, 20x4

Revenues

Expenses

Net income

Hartford Go-Cart Lanes
Statement of Owner's Equity
For the Year Ended December 31, 20x4

Chapter 4, P 6. (Continued)

Hartford Go-Cart Lanes
Balance Sheet
December 31, 20x4

Assets

Liabilities

Owner's Equity

4. Reason for closing entries explained

Chapter 4, P 7.

1. Closing entries prepared

Chapter 4, P 7. (Continued)

2. Income statement, statement of owner's equity, and balance sheet prepared

Revenues

Expenses

Net income

(continued)

Chapter 4, P 7. (Continued)

Assets		
Liabilities		
Owner's Equity		

Chapter 4, P 8.
1. Work sheet completed

Flynn Theater
Work Sheet
For the Year Ended December 31, 20x5

Account Name	Trial Balance Debit	Trial Balance Credit	Adjustments Debit	Adjustments Credit	Adjusted Trial Balance Debit	Adjusted Trial Balance Credit	Income Statement Debit	Income Statement Credit	Balance Sheet Debit	Balance Sheet Credit
Cash	15,900									
Accounts Receivable	9,272									
Prepaid Insurance	9,800									
Office Supplies	390									
Cleaning Supplies	1,795									
Land	10,000									
Building	200,000									
Accumulated Depreciation, Building		19,700								
Theater Furnishings	185,000									
Accumulated Depreciation, Theater Furnishings		32,500								
Office Equipment	15,800									
Accumulated Depreciation, Office Equipment		7,780									
Accounts Payable		22,753								
Gift Books Liability		20,950								
Mortgage Payable		150,000								
Danielle Flynn, Capital		156,324								
Danielle Flynn, Withdrawals	30,000									
Ticket Sales Revenue		205,700								
Theater Rental		22,600								
Usher Wages Expense	92,000									
Office Wages Expense	12,000									
Utilities Expense	56,350									
	638,307	638,307								
Net Income										

Chapter 4, P 8. (Continued)

2. Income statement, statement of owner's equity, and balance sheet prepared

Flynn Theater
Income Statement
For the Year Ended December 31, 20x5

Revenues

Expenses

Net income

Flynn Theater
Statement of Owner's Equity
For the Year Ended December 31, 20x5

Chapter 4, P 8. (Continued)

Flynn Theater
Balance Sheet
December 31, 20x5

Assets

Liabilities

Owner's Equity

Chapter 4, P 8. (Continued)

3. Adjusting, closing, and reversing entries prepared

Chapter 4, P 8. (Continued)

Chapter 4, SD 1.

Chapter 4, SD 3.

Chapter 4, SD 5.

1. Statement of cash receipts and expenditures prepared

Adele's Secretarial Service
Statement of Cash Receipts and Expenditures
For the Year Ended June 30, 20x4

Cash receipts from customers	$22,460	[a]
Cash expenditures		
Increase in cash		

Explanations

a.

b.

c.

d.

Chapter 4, SD 5. (Continued)

2. Memorandum explaining balance sheet changes and treatment of depreciation expense prepared

Memorandum

Date:
To:
From:
Re:

Chapter 4, FRA 1.

1. Closing entries prepared

(numbers are in thousands)

Service Revenues	2,333,064	

2.

Chapter 4, FRA 2.

Chapter 4, FRA 3.

Chapter 4, FRA 4.

(in millions)	Quarter				Total
	1st	2nd	3rd	4th	
Walgreens					
Net Sales					
Percentages					
Net Earnings					
Percentages					*
Toys "R" Us					
Net Sales					
Percentages					
Net Earnings (Loss)					
Percentages					*

*Rounded.

Comprehensive Problem: Joan Miller Advertising Agency

1. Reversing entries prepared and posted
2 and 3. Transactions for August journalized and posted
7 and 8. Adjusting and closing entries prepared and posted

General Journal   Page

Date		Description	Post. Ref.	Debit	Credit
		Reversing entries			
20xx					
Aug.	1	Wages Payable		360	
		Wages Expense			360
		Reversed the adjusting entry			
		for accrued wages			
		Transactions for August			

Comprehensive Problem: Joan Miller Advertising Agency (Continued)

General Journal

Page

Date	Description	Post. Ref.	Debit	Credit
20xx				

Comprehensive Problem: Joan Miller Advertising Agency (Continued)

Date	Description	Post. Ref.	Debit	Credit
20xx				

Comprehensive Problem: Joan Miller Advertising Agency (Continued)

General Journal

Page

Date	Description	Post. Ref.	Debit	Credit
20xx				

Comprehensive Problem: Joan Miller Advertising Agency (Continued)

Date	Description	Post. Ref.	Debit	Credit
20xx				

Comprehensive Problem: Joan Miller Advertising Agency (Continued)

Date	Description	Post. Ref.	Debit	Credit
20xx				

Comprehensive Problem: Joan Miller Advertising Agency (Continued)

General Ledger

Cash — Account No. 111

Date		Item	Post. Ref.	Debit	Credit	Balance Debit	Balance Credit
20xx							
July	1		J1	20,000		20,000	
	2		J1		1,600	18,400	
	4		J1		4,200	14,200	
	5		J1		1,500	12,700	
	8		J1		960	11,740	
	9		J1		1,000	10,740	
	10		J2	1,400		12,140	
	12		J2		1,200	10,940	
	15		J2	1,000		11,940	
	26		J2		1,200	10,740	
	29		J2		200	10,540	
	31		J2		1,400	9,140	
Aug.	1		J5	6,300		15,440	

Comprehensive Problem: Joan Miller Advertising Agency (Continued)

Accounts Receivable — Account No. 113

Date		Item	Post. Ref.	Debit	Credit	Balance Debit	Balance Credit
20xx							
July	19		J2	4,800		4,800	
	31	Adj. (i)	J3	200		5,000	

Art Supplies — Account No. 115

Date		Item	Post. Ref.	Debit	Credit	Balance Debit	Balance Credit
20xx							
July	6		J1	1,800		1,800	
	31	Adj. (c)	J3		500	1,300	

Office Supplies — Account No. 116

Date		Item	Post. Ref.	Debit	Credit	Balance Debit	Balance Credit
20xx							
July	6		J1	800		800	
	31	Adj. (d)	J3		200	600	

Comprehensive Problem: Joan Miller Advertising Agency (Continued)

Prepaid Rent — Account No. 117

Date		Item	Post. Ref.	Debit	Credit	Balance Debit	Balance Credit
20xx							
July	2		J1	1,600		1,600	
	31	Adj. (a)	J3		800	800	

Prepaid Insurance — Account No. 118

Date		Item	Post. Ref.	Debit	Credit	Balance Debit	Balance Credit
20xx							
July	8		J1	960		960	
	31	Adj. (b)	J3		80	880	

Art Equipment — Account No. 144

Date		Item	Post. Ref.	Debit	Credit	Balance Debit	Balance Credit
20xx							
July	4		J1	4,200		4,200	

Accumulated Depreciation, Art Equipment — Account No. 145

Date		Item	Post. Ref.	Debit	Credit	Balance Debit	Balance Credit
20xx							
July	31	Adj. (e)	J3		70		70

Comprehensive Problem: Joan Miller Advertising Agency (Continued)

Office Equipment   Account No. 146

Date		Item	Post. Ref.	Debit	Credit	Balance Debit	Balance Credit
20xx							
July	5		J1	3,000		3,000	

Accumulated Depreciation, Office Equipment   Account No. 147

Date		Item	Post. Ref.	Debit	Credit	Balance Debit	Balance Credit
20xx							
July	31	Adj. (f)	J3		50		50

Accounts Payable   Account No. 212

Date		Item	Post. Ref.	Debit	Credit	Balance Debit	Balance Credit
20xx							
July	5		J1		1,500		1,500
	6		J1		2,600		4,100
	9		J1	1,000			3,100
	30		J2		140		3,240

Comprehensive Problem: Joan Miller Advertising Agency (Continued)

Unearned Art Fees — Account No. 213

Date		Item	Post. Ref.	Debit	Credit	Balance Debit	Balance Credit
20xx							
July	15		J2		1,000		1,000
	31	Adj. (h)	J3	400			600

Wages Payable — Account No. 214

Date		Item	Post. Ref.	Debit	Credit	Balance Debit	Balance Credit
20xx							
July	31	Adj. (g)	J3		360		360

Joan Miller, Capital — Account No. 311

Date		Item	Post. Ref.	Debit	Credit	Balance Debit	Balance Credit
20xx							
July	1		J1		20,000		20,000
	31	Closing	J4		2,000		22,000
	31	Closing	J4	1,400			20,600

Comprehensive Problem: Joan Miller Advertising Agency (Continued)

Joan Miller, Withdrawals — Account No. 312

Date		Item	Post. Ref.	Debit	Credit	Balance Debit	Balance Credit
20xx							
July	31		J2	1,400		1,400	
	31	Closing	J4		1,400	—	

Income Summary — Account No. 313

Date		Item	Post. Ref.	Debit	Credit	Balance Debit	Balance Credit
20xx							
July	31	Closing	J4		6,800		6,800
	31	Closing	J4	4,800			2,000
	31	Closing	J4	2,000			—

Advertising Fees Earned — Account No. 411

Date		Item	Post. Ref.	Debit	Credit	Balance Debit	Balance Credit
20xx							
July	10		J2		1,400		1,400
	19		J2		4,800		6,200
	31	Adj. (i)	J3		200		6,400
	31	Closing	J4	6,400			—

Comprehensive Problem: Joan Miller Advertising Agency (Continued)

Art Fees Earned — Account No. 412

Date		Item	Post. Ref.	Debit	Credit	Balance Debit	Balance Credit
20xx							
July	31	Adj. (h)	J3		400		400
	31	Closing	J4	400			—

Wages Expense — Account No. 511

Date		Item	Post. Ref.	Debit	Credit	Balance Debit	Balance Credit
20xx							
July	12		J2	1,200		1,200	
	26		J2	1,200		2,400	
	31	Adj. (g)	J3	360		2,760	
	31	Closing	J4		2,760	—	

Utilities Expense — Account No. 512

Date		Item	Post. Ref.	Debit	Credit	Balance Debit	Balance Credit
20xx							
July	29		J2	200		200	
	31	Closing	J4		200	—	

Comprehensive Problem: Joan Miller Advertising Agency (Continued)

Telephone Expense — Account No. 513

Date		Item	Post. Ref.	Debit	Credit	Balance Debit	Balance Credit
20xx							
July	30		J2	140		140	
	31	Closing	J4		140	—	

Rent Expense — Account No. 514

Date		Item	Post. Ref.	Debit	Credit	Balance Debit	Balance Credit
20xx							
July	31	Adj. (a)	J3	800		800	
	31	Closing	J4		800	—	

Insurance Expense — Account No. 515

Date		Item	Post. Ref.	Debit	Credit	Balance Debit	Balance Credit
20xx							
July	31	Adj. (b)	J3	80		80	
	31	Closing	J4		80	—	

Art Supplies Expense — Account No. 516

Date		Item	Post. Ref.	Debit	Credit	Balance Debit	Balance Credit
20xx							
July	31	Adj. (c)	J3	500		500	
	31	Closing	J4		500	—	

Comprehensive Problem: Joan Miller Advertising Agency (Continued)

Office Supplies Expense Account No. 517

Date		Item	Post. Ref.	Debit	Credit	Balance Debit	Balance Credit
20xx							
July	31	Adj. (d)	J3	200		200	
	31	Closing	J4		200	—	

Depreciation Expense, Art Equipment Account No. 519

Date		Item	Post. Ref.	Debit	Credit	Balance Debit	Balance Credit
20xx							
July	31	Adj. (e)	J3	70		70	
	31	Closing	J4		70	—	

Depreciation Expense, Office Equipment Account No. 520

Date		Item	Post. Ref.	Debit	Credit	Balance Debit	Balance Credit
20xx							
July	31	Adj. (f)	J3	50		50	
	31	Closing	J4		50	—	

Comprehensive Problem: Joan Miller Advertising Agency (Continued)

4 and 5. Trial balance and work sheet prepared

Joan Miller Advertising Agency
Work Sheet
For the Month Ended August 31, 20xx

Account Name	Trial Balance Debit	Trial Balance Credit	Adjustments Debit	Adjustments Credit	Adjusted Trial Balance Debit	Adjusted Trial Balance Credit	Income Statement Debit	Income Statement Credit	Balance Sheet Debit	Balance Sheet Credit
Cash	13,770				13,770				13,770	
Net Income										

Comprehensive Problem: Joan Miller Advertising Agency (Continued)		
6. Income statement, statement of owner's equity, and balance sheet prepared		
Joan Miller Advertising Agency **Income Statement** **For the Month Ended August 31, 20xx**		
Revenues		
Expenses		
Net income		
Joan Miller Advertising Agency **Statement of Owner's Equity** **For the Month Ended August 31, 20xx**		

Comprehensive Problem: Joan Miller Advertising Agency (Continued)

Joan Miller Advertising Agency
Balance Sheet
August 31, 20xx

Assets

Cash		$13,770

Liabilities

Owner's Equity

Comprehensive Problem: Joan Miller Advertising Agency (Continued)

9. Post-closing trial balance prepared

Joan Miller Advertising Agency
Post-Closing Trial Balance
August 31, 20xx

Cash	$13,770	

Chapter 5, SE 1.

1.
2.
3.
4.

Chapter 5, SE 2.

Martin's Hardware
Income Statement
For the Month Ended February 28, 20xx

Net sales		$50,000

Chapter 5, SE 3.

List price	
Less 40 percent	
Dealer price	
Shipping cost	
Cost of tooling machine	
Less sales discount	
Net cost of tooling machine	

Chapter 5, SE 4.

Apr.	19			

Chapter 5, SE 5.

Aug.	2			

Chapter 5, SE 6.

Aug.	4			

Chapter 5, SE 7.

Chapter 5, SE 8.

Purchases: $238,000			
Cost of goods sold			
Merchandise inventory,			
Sept. 30, 20xx		$ 33,000	

Chapter 5, SE 9.

Chapter 5, SE 10.

1. **The perpetual inventory system**

2. **The periodic inventory system**

Chapter 5, SE 11.

Farid Company records:

Smarte Company records:

Chapter 5, E 1.

1:
2.
3.
4.
5.
6.

Chapter 5, E 2.

1. Operating report prepared

Pacific Hardware Company
Operating Budget
For the Six Months Ended June 30, 20x3

	Budget	Actual	Difference Under (Over) Budget
Operating expenses			
Selling expenses			
Sales salaries expense	$ 90,000	$102,030	$(12,030)
Sales supplies expense	2,000	1,642	358
Rent expense, selling space	18,000	18,000	—
Utilities expense, selling space	12,000	11,256	744
Advertising expense	15,000	21,986	(6,986)
Depreciation expense, selling fixtures	6,500	6,778	(278)
Total selling expenses	$143,500	$161,692	$(18,192)
General and administrative expenses			
Office salaries expense	$ 50,000	$ 47,912	$ 2,088
Office supplies expense	1,000	782	218
Rent expense, office space	4,000	4,000	—
Depreciation expense, office equipment	3,000	3,251	(251)
Utilities expense, office space	3,000	3,114	(114)
Postage expense	500	626	(126)
Insurance expense	2,000	2,700	(700)
Miscellaneous expense	500	481	19
Total general and administrative expenses	$ 64,000	$ 62,866	$ 1,134
Total operating expenses	$207,500	$224,558	$(17,058)

Chapter 5, E 2. (Continued)

2. Operating budget discussed

Chapter 5, E 3.

Sales		Cost of Goods Sold	Gross Margin		Operating Expenses		Net Income (Loss)
$250,000		(a)	$ 80,000			(b)	$ 24,000
	(c)	216,000	120,000		80,000		40,000
460,000		(d)	100,000			(e)	(2,000)
780,000		(f)		(g)	240,000		80,000

Chapter 5, E 4.

List price	
Less 30 percent	
Dealer price	
Shipping cost	
Cost of refrigerator	
Less sales discount	
Net cost of refrigerator	

Chapter 5, E 5.

City Rental
Income Statement
For the Year Ended December 31, 20xx

Net sales		
Gross sales		$237,500

	Chapter 5, E 6.		
a.	Merchandise Inventory	2,500	
	Accounts Payable		2,500
	Purchased merchandise, terms n/30, FOB		
	shipping point		
b.			
c.			
d.			
e.			
f.			
g.			
h.			

Chapter 5, E 7.

June	15	Accounts Receivable	1,300	
		Sales		1,300
		Sold merchandise to Whist Company, terms n/30		

Chapter 5, E 8.

Atlanta General Store
Income Statement
For the Year Ended December 31, 20x4

Net sales			
Gross sales			$594,000

Chapter 5, E 9.

	20x4	20x3	20x2
Gross sales	(o)	(h)	$286
Sales returns and allowances	24	19	(a)
Net sales	(p)	317	(b)
Merchandise inventory, beginning	(q)	(i)	38
Purchases	192	169	(c)
Purchases returns and allowances	31	(j)	17
Freight in	(r)	29	22
Net cost of purchases	189	(k)	(d)
Goods available for sale	222	212	182
Merchandise inventory, ending	39	(l)	42
Cost of goods sold	(s)	179	(e)
Gross margin	142	(m)	126
Selling expenses	(t)	78	(f)
General and administrative expenses	39	(n)	33
Total operating expenses	130	128	(g)
Net income	(u)	10	27

Chapter 5, E 10.

a.	Purchases	2,500	
	Accounts Payable		2,500
	Purchased merchandise, terms n/30, FOB shipping point		
b.			
c.			
d.			
e.			
f.			
g.			
h.			

Chapter 5, E 11.

June	15				

Chapter 5, E 12.

20xx					
Dec.	31				

Chapter 5, E 13.

20xx				
Dec.	31			

Chapter 5, E 14.

Mar.				

Chapter 5, E 15.

July	2				
July	2				

Chapter 5, E 16.

1. Entries prepared by the Melody Company

2. Entries prepared by the Mirro Company

Chapter 5, P 1.

1. Income statement prepared

Bear Camera Store
Income Statement
For the Year Ended June 30, 20x4

Net sales			
Gross sales			$433,912

Chapter 5, P 1. (Continued)

2. Income statement discussed

Chapter 5, P 2.

1. Transactions recorded

20xx				

Chapter 5, P 2. (Continued)

20xx				

2. Purchase transactions discussed

Chapter 5, P 3.

1. Income statement prepared

Pat's Sports Equipment
Income Statement
For the Year Ended September 30, 20x5

Net sales			
Gross sales			$1,301,736

Chapter 5, P 3. (Continued)

2. Income statement discussed

Chapter 5, P 4.				
20xx				
July	1	Accounts Receivable	4,200	
		Sales		4,200
		Sold merchandise to Rick Lee, terms		
		n/30, FOB shipping point		

Chapter 5, P 4. (Continued)

20xx				

Chapter 5, P 5.

1. Work sheet completed

Account Name	Trial Balance Debit	Trial Balance Credit	Adjustments Debit	Adjustments Credit	Income Statement Debit	Income Statement Credit	Balance Sheet Debit	Balance Sheet Credit
Cash	7,050						7,050	
Accounts Receivable	24,830							
Merchandise Inventory	88,900							
Store Supplies	3,800							
Prepaid Insurance	4,800							
Store Equipment	151,300							
Accumulated Depreciation, Store Equipment		25,500						
Accounts Payable		38,950						
Jarrott Clay, Capital		161,350						
Jarrott Clay, Withdrawals	24,000							
Sales		475,250						
Sales Returns and Allowances	4,690							
Cost of Goods Sold	231,840							
Freight In	10,400							
Sales Salaries Expense	64,600							
Rent Expense	48,000							
Other Selling Expenses	32,910							
Utilities Expense	3,930							
	701,050	701,050						
Net Income								

Chapter 5, P 5. (Continued)

2. Income statement, statement of owner's equity, and balance sheet prepared

Chapter 5, P 5. (Continued)

Assets

Liabilities

Owner's Equity

Chapter 5, P 5. (Continued)

3. Closing entries prepared

20x4

Chapter 5, P 6.

1. Work sheet completed

East End Bookstore
Work Sheet
For the Year Ended June 30, 20x3

Account Name	Trial Balance		Adjustments		Income Statement		Balance Sheet	
	Debit	Credit	Debit	Credit	Debit	Credit	Debit	Credit
Net Income								

Chapter 5, P 6. (Continued)

2. Income statement, statement of owner's equity, and balance sheet prepared

East End Bookstore
Income Statement
For the Year Ended June 30, 20x3

Net sales			
Gross sales			$102,250
Net income			

Chapter 5, P 6. (Continued)

East End Bookstore
Statement of Owner's Equity
For the Year Ended June 30, 20x3

East End Bookstore
Balance Sheet
June 30, 20x3

Assets

Liabilities

Owner's Equity

Chapter 5, P 6. (Continued)

3.	Closing entries prepared			
20x3				
June	**30**			

Chapter 5, P 7.

20xx				
Jan.	2			

Chapter 5, P 7. (Continued)

20xx				

Chapter 5, P 7. (Continued)

Chapter 5, P 7. (Continued)

20xx				

Chapter 5, P 7. (Continued)

Chapter 5, P 7. (Continued)

20xx				

Chapter 5, P 8.

1. Income statement prepared

<table>
<tr><td colspan="4" align="center">Holiday Merchandise
Income Statement
For the Year Ended August 31, 20x4</td></tr>
<tr><td>Net sales</td><td></td><td></td><td></td></tr>
<tr><td> Gross sales</td><td></td><td></td><td>$324,000</td></tr>
</table>

Chapter 5, P 8. (Continued)

2. Income statement discussed

Chapter 5, P 9.

1. Transactions recorded

20x4					
Oct.	7	Accounts Receivable		6,000	
		Sales			6,000
		Sold merchandise to Sonia Mendes,			
		terms n/30, FOB shipping point			

Chapter 5, P 9. (Continued)

20x4				

2. Purchase transactions discussed

Chapter 5, P 9. (Continued)

Chapter 5, P 10.

1. Income statement prepared

Gourmet Gadgets Shop
Income Statement
For the Year Ended March 31, 20x4

Chapter 5, P 10. (Continued)

2. Income statement discussed

Chapter 5, P 11.

20x4				

Chapter 5, P 11.

Chapter 5, P 11. (Continued)

20x4				

Chapter 5, SD 1.

Chapter 5, SD 2.

The Periodic Inventory System

The Perpetual Inventory System

Chapter 5, SD 2. (Continued)

Chapter 5, SD 3.

The aspects of the practice are as follows:

1.

2.

Chapter 5, SD 5.

1. Cost of goods sold recomputed

	20x6	20x5
Beginning inventory	$ 53,000	
Purchases		
Less purchases allowances		
Net purchases		
Freight in		
Net cost of purchases		
Goods available for sale		
Less ending inventory		
Cost of goods sold		

20x6 net income		
Manager's salary		
Inventory loss		
20x5 net income		

2. Possible reasons for the inventory loss suggested

Chapter 5, FRA 1.

1.

	Wal-Mart		Kmart	
	(millions)	%	(millions)	%
Net sales		100.0%		100.0%
Cost of goods sold				
Gross margin				
Operating expenses				
Income from operations				
Inventory				
Inventory/cost of goods sold				

2.

3.

Chapter 5, FRA 2.

The reasons for the English use of terminology are as follows:

Profit and loss account

Turnover

Stocks

Debtors

Creditors

Chapter 5, FRA 3.

Memorandum

Date:	Today's Date
To:	Instructor's Name
From:	Student's Name
Re:	Toys "R" Us's Operating Cycle and Financing Period

Chapter 5, FRA 4.

(Dollars in millions)	Toys "R" Us		Walgreens	
	2002	%	2001	%
Net sales				
Cost of sales				
Gross margin				
Total operating expenses				
Income from operations				
Inventory				

Chapter 6, SE 1.

1.
2.
3.
4.
5.

Chapter 6, SE 2.

1.
2.
3.
4.
5.

Chapter 6, SE 3.

1.
2.
3.
4.
5.
6.
7.
8.
9.
10.

Chapter 6, SE 4.

Balance Sheet
May 31, 20xx
Assets

Liabilities

Owner's Equity

Chapter 6, SE 5.

1.
2.
3.
4.
5.
6.
7.
8.

Chapter 6, SE 6.

Income Statement		
For the Year Ended May 31, 20xx		

Chapter 6, SE 7.

Income Statement
For the Year Ended May 31, 20xx

Chapter 6, SE 8.

Current Assets =

=

Working Capital = —

=

Current Ratio = =

Chapter 6, SE 9.

1. Profit Margin = =

2. Asset Turnover = =

3. Return on Assets = =

4. Debt to Equity Ratio = =

5. Return on Equity = =

Chapter 6, E 1.

1.		12.	
2.		13.	
3.		14.	
4.		15.	
5.		16.	
6.		17.	
7.		18.	
8.		19.	
9.		20.	
10.		21.	
11.		22.	

Chapter 6, E 2.

1.	
2.	
3.	
4.	
5.	

Chapter 6, E 3.

1.		9.	
2.		10.	
3.		11.	
4.		12.	
5.		13.	
6.		14.	
7.		15.	
8.		16.	

Chapter 6, E 4.

Assets

Liabilities

Stockholders' Equity

Chapter 6, E 5.

1.		9.	
2.		10.	
3.		11.	
4.		12.	
5.		13.	
6.		14.	
7.		15.	
8.		16.	

Chapter 6, E 6.

1. Single-step income statement prepared

2. Multistep income statement prepared

Chapter 6, E 7.

Harrington Housewares Company
Income Statement
For the Year Ended June 30, 20xx

Chapter 6, E 8.

1. Working capital computed

Current Assets

Current Liabilities

Working Capital

2. Current ratio computed

Current Ratio =

Chapter 6, E 9.

1. Profit Margin	=	
2. Asset Turnover	=	
3. Return on Assets	=	
4. Debt to Equity Ratio	=	
5. Return on Equity	=	

Chapter 6, E 10.

1. Liquidity measures computed

a.	Current Assets	
	Current Liabilities	
	Working Capital	
b.	Current Ratio	=

2. Profitability measures computed

a.	Profit Margin	=
b.	Asset Turnover	=
c.	Return on Assets	=
d.	Debt to Equity Ratio	=
e.	Return on Equity	=

Chapter 6, P 1.

1.
2.
3.
4.
5.

Chapter 6, P 2.

1a. Detailed income statement prepared

Inge Robotics Company
Income Statement
For the Year Ended July 31, 20x5

Sales				$922,200

Chapter 6, P 2. (Continued)

1b. **Condensed multistep income statement prepared**

Inge Robotics Company
Income Statement
For the Year Ended July 31, 20x5

Net sales		$868,400

1c. **Condensed single-step income statement prepared**

Inge Robotics Company
Income Statement
For the Year Ended July 31, 20x5

Chapter 6, P 2. (Continued)

2. Usefulness of income statement forms discussed

Chapter 6, P 3.

Theopoulos Machine Company
Balance Sheet
July 31, 20x4

Assets

Current assets

  Cash $ 31,000

(continued)

Chapter 6, P 3. (Continued)

Liabilities		
Owner's Equity		

Chapter 6, P 4.

1. Liquidity measures computed and discussed

a. Working Capital

	20x4	20x3
Current Assets		
Current Liabilities		
Working Capital		

b. Current Ratio =

20x4:

20x3:

2. Profitability measures computed and discussed

a. Profit Margin =

20x4:

20x3:

Chapter 6, P 4. (Continued)

b.	**Asset Turnover**	=	
	20x4:		
	20x3:		
c.	**Return on Assets**	=	
	20x4:		
	20x3:		
d.	**Debt to Equity Ratio**	=	
	20x4:		
	20x3:		
e.	**Return on Equity**	=	
	20x4:		
	20x3:		

Chapter 6, P 5.

1a. Single-step income statement prepared

Folino Company
Income Statement
For the Year Ended December 31, 20x6

1b. Statement of owner's equity prepared

Folino Company
Statement of Owner's Equity
For the Year Ended December 31, 20x6

Chapter 6, P 5. (Continued)

1c. Classified balance sheet prepared

<table>
<tr><td colspan="4" align="center">**Folino Company**
Balance Sheet
December 31, 20x6</td></tr>
<tr><td colspan="4" align="center">**Assets**</td></tr>
<tr><td>**Current assets**</td><td></td><td></td><td></td></tr>
<tr><td> Cash</td><td></td><td>$ 56,800</td><td></td></tr>
<tr><td colspan="4" align="center">**Liabilities**</td></tr>
<tr><td colspan="4" align="center">**Owner's Equity**</td></tr>
</table>

Chapter 6, P 5. (Continued)

2a. Liquidity measures computed

Current Assets	
Current Liabilities	
Working Capital	

Current Ratio = ―――― =

2b. Profitability measures computed

Profit Margin = ―――― =

Asset Turnover = ――――

=

Return on Assets = ――――

=

Debt to Equity Ratio = ―――― =

Return on Equity = ――――

=

Chapter 6, P 5. (Continued)

3.

Chapter 6, P 6.

1.

2.

3.

4.

5.

Chapter 6, P 7.

1a. Detailed income statement prepared

Sales			$541,230

Chapter 6, P 7. (Continued)

1b. Condensed multistep income statement prepared

Net sales		$525,932

1c. Condensed single-step income statement prepared

Chapter 6, P 7. (Continued)

2. Usefulness of income statement forms discussed

Chapter 6, P 8.

1. Liquidity measures computed and discussed

a. Working Capital

	20x5	20x4
Current Assets		
Current Liabilities		
Working Capital		

b. Current Ratio =

20x5:

20x4:

2. Profitability measures computed and discussed

a. Profit Margin =

20x5:

20x4:

Chapter 6, P 8. (Continued)

b. Asset Turnover =

20x5:

20x4:

c. Return on Assets =

20x5:

20x4:

d. Debt to Equity Ratio =

20x5:

20x4:

e. Return on Equity =

20x5:

20x4:

Chapter 6, SD 1.

Chapter 6, SD 2.

Chapter 6, SD 3.

Chapter 6, SD 4.

Chapter 6, SD 6.

1. Analysis performed

Analysis of Handy Harvey Company

	Before Loan	After Loan
Liquidity		
Working Capital		
Current Ratio		
Profitability		
Profit Margin		
Asset Turnover		
Return on Assets		
Debt to Equity Ratio		
Return on Equity		

Discussion

Chapter 6, SD 6. (Continued)

Analysis of Sheila's Fashions

		Before Loan	After Loan
Liquidity			
	Working Capital		
	Current Ratio		
Profitability			
	Profit Margin		
	Asset Turnover		
	Return on Assets		
	Debt to Equity Ratio		
	Return on Equity		

Discussion

Chapter 6, SD 6. (Continued)

2. Loan decision recommendation made

Memorandum

Date:
To:
From:
Re:

Chapter 6, FRA 1.

1. Profitability ratios computed (in millions) and discussed

	Albertson's	A&P
Net Income	$765	$14
Net Sales		
Profit Margin		
Net Sales		
Average Total Assets		
Asset Turnover		
Net Income		
Average Total Assets (from above)		
Return on Assets		
Total Liabilities		
Total Stockholders' Equity		
Debt to Equity Ratio		
Net Income		
Average Stockholders' Equity		
Return on Equity		

Chapter 6, FRA 1. (Continued)

2. Return on assets discussed

3. Debt financing discussed

Chapter 6, FRA 2.

Profit margin and return on assets computed:

Profit Margin =

20x4:

20x3:

Return on Assets =

20x4:

20x3:

Chapter 6, FRA 2. (Continued)

Asset turnover computed:

$$\text{Asset Turnover} = \frac{}{}$$

20x4: =

20x3: =

Comment on performance:

Chapter 6, FRA 3.

1. Liquidity and profitability measures computed (amounts in millions)

		2002	2001	2001–2002 Industry
	Current Assets			
	Current Liabilities			
	Working Capital			
Current Ratio =	Current Assets / Current Liabilities			
Profit Margin =				
Asset Turnover =				
Return on Assets =				
Debt to Equity Ratio =				
Return on Equity =				NA

Chapter 6, FRA 3. (Continued)

2. Executive Summary memorandum prepared

Memorandum

Date:
To:
From:
Re:

Chapter 6, FRA 4.

1. Components of U.K. balance sheet identified and discussed

U.K. Balance Sheet Term	U.S. Balance Sheet Term

Chapter 6, FRA 4. (Continued)

2. Ratios computed

British pound amounts are in millions

Current Ratio: Current Assets divided by Creditors: Amounts Due Within One Year

1999:

2000:

Debt to Equity Ratio: (Creditors: Amounts Due Within One Year + Long-Term Liabilities) divided by Capital Employed

1999:

2000:

Return on Assets: Net Income divided by (Fixed Assets + Current Assets)

1999:

2000:

Return on Equity: Net Income divided by Capital Employed

1999:

2000:

Chapter 6, FRA 5.

1. Consolidated balance sheets

a. Working capital

	2002	2001	Increase (Decrease)
Current Assets			
Current Liabilities			
Working Capital			

b. Current ratio

Current Ratio =

2002:   2001:

c.

d. Debt to equity ratio

Debt to Equity Ratio =

2002:   2001:

e.

Chapter 6, FRA 5. (Continued)

2. Consolidated statements of earnings

a.

b.

c.

d.

e.

Profit Margin =

2002:   2001:

f.

Asset Turnover =

2002:

2001:

Chapter 6, FRA 5. (Continued)

g.

Return on Assets =

2002:

2001:

h.

Return on Equity =

2002:

2001:

Chapter 6, FRA 5. (Continued)

3. Multistep income statements prepared and discussed

Toys "R" Us, Inc.
Consolidated Statements of Earnings
For the Years Ended February 1, 2003, and February 2, 2002
(in thousands)

	2002		2001	
	Amount	Percentage	Amount	Percentage
Net sales	$11,305,000	100.0%	$11,019,000	100.0%

Comment on performance:

Chapter 6, FRA 6.

Working Capital:

Walgreens

	2002	2001	Increase (Decrease)
Current Assets			
Current Liabilities			
Working Capital			

Toys "R" Us

	2002	2001	Increase (Decrease)
Current Assets			
Current Liabilities			
Working Capital			

Current Ratio:

Current Ratio =

Walgreens

2002:		2001:	

Toys "R" Us

2002:		2001:	

Debt to Equity Ratio:

Debt to Equity Ratio =

Walgreens

2002:		2001:	

Toys "R" Us

2002:		2001:	

Chapter 6, FRA 6. (Continued)

Profit Margin:

Profit Margin = _____

Walgreens

2002: _____ = _____   2001: _____ = _____

Toys "R" Us

2002: _____ = _____   2001: _____ = _____

Asset Turnover:

Asset Turnover = _____

Walgreens

2002:

2001:

Toys "R" Us

2002:

2001:

Chapter 6, FRA 6. (Continued)

Return on Assets:

Return on Assets =

Walgreens

2002:

2001:

Toys "R" Us

2002:

2001:

Return on Equity:

Return on Equity =

Walgreens

2002:

2001:

Toys "R" Us

2002:

2001:

Chapter 7, SE 1.

1.		3.	
2.		4.	

Chapter 7, SE 2.

1.		4.	
2.		5.	
3.		6.	

Chapter 7, SE 3.

Chapter 7, SE 4.

1.		4.	
2.		5.	
3.		6.	

Chapter 7, SE 5.

Sales Journal

Date	Account Debited	Invoice Number	Post. Ref.	Amount (Debit Accounts Receivable/ Credit Sales)
20xx				

Chapter 7, SE 6.

Chapter 7, SE 7.

Purchases Journal

Date	Account Credited	Date of Invoice	Terms	Post. Ref.	Credit — Accounts Payable	Debits — Purchases	Debits — Freight In	Debits — Store Supplies	Debits — Office Supplies	Other Accounts — Account	Other Accounts — Post. Ref.	Other Accounts — Amount
20xx												

Chapter 7, SE 8.

Chapter 7, SE 9.

Cash Receipts Journal

Date	Account Debited/Credited	Post. Ref.	Debits			Credits		
			Cash	Sales Discounts	Other Accounts	Accounts Receivable	Sales	Other Accounts
20xx								

Chapter 7, SE 10.

			Cash Payments Journal			Credits		Debits	
Date	Ck. No.	Payee	Account Credited/Debited	Post. Ref.	Cash	Purchases Discounts	Other Accounts	Accounts Payable	Other Accounts
20xx									

Chapter 7, E 1.

1.
2.
3.
4.
5.
6.
7.
8.
9.
10.
11.
12.

Chapter 7, E 2.

1.

Chapter 7, E 3.

1.
2. May 25:
3.
   a.
   b.
   c.
   d.

Chapter 7, E 4.

1. Purchases journal set up
2. Transactions entered, and columns footed and crossfooted

Purchases Journal
Page 1

Date		Account Credited	Date of Invoice	Terms	Post. Ref.	Credit – Accounts Payable	Debits – Purchases	Debits – Freight In	Debits – Store Supplies	Debits – Office Supplies	Other Accounts – Account	Other Accounts – Post. Ref.	Other Accounts – Amount
July	1	Burlington Company	7/1	2/10, n/30		5,400	5,400						
		Debit Column Totals								Credit Column Totals			

Chapter 7, E 5.

1.
2.
3.
4.
5.

Chapter 7, E 6.

1. Ledger accounts opened and amounts posted from the sales journal

General Ledger

Accounts Receivable — Account No. 112

Date	Item	Post. Ref.	Debit	Credit	Balance Debit	Balance Credit

Sales — Account No. 411

Date	Item	Post. Ref.	Debit	Credit	Balance Debit	Balance Credit

Accounts Receivable Subsidiary Ledger

Ed Kohen

Date	Item	Post. Ref.	Debit	Credit	Balance

Sue Longo

Date	Item	Post. Ref.	Debit	Credit	Balance

Chapter 7, E 6. (Continued)

Ye Tang

Date	Item	Post. Ref.	Debit	Credit	Balance

Gina Touloumos

Date	Item	Post. Ref.	Debit	Credit	Balance

2. Accounts receivable subsidiary ledger proved

Total Accounts Receivable	

Chapter 7, E 7.

1. Sales account entries identified

Oct.	31	
	31	
	31	

2. M. Kern entries identified

Oct.	8	
	12	
	18	

Chapter 7, E 8.

1. D. Amir's transactions identified

Mar.	31	
Apr.	7	
	12	
Apr.	17	

2. Wong Company transactions identified

Apr.	18	
	20	
	25	

Chapter 7, P 1.

1. Special-purpose journals and general journal prepared
5. Transactions entered in journals
6. Journals footed and crossfooted

Sales Journal						Page 1
Date	Account Debited	Invoice Number	Terms	Post. Ref.	Debit Accounts Receivable/ Credit Sales	
May 2						

Chapter 7, P 1. (Continued)

Purchases Journal — Page 1

Date	Account Credited	Date of Invoice	Terms	Post. Ref.	Debit Purchases/ Credit Accounts Payable

Cash Receipts Journal — Page 1

Date	Account Debited/Credited	Post. Ref.	Debits		Credits		
			Cash	Sales Discounts	Accounts Receivable	Sales	Other Accounts

Cash Payments Journal — Page 1

Date	Ck. No.	Payee	Account Credited/Debited	Post. Ref.	Credits		Debits	
					Cash	Purchases Discounts	Accounts Payable	Other Accounts

Chapter 7, P 1. (Continued)

General Journal   Page 1

Date	Description	Post. Ref.	Debit	Credit
May 8				

2. General ledger accounts opened
5. Transactions posted
6. End-of-month postings made

General Ledger

Accounts Receivable   Account No. 112

Date	Item	Post. Ref.	Debit	Credit	Balance Debit	Balance Credit
Apr. 30	Balance					

Accounts Payable   Account No. 211

Date	Item	Post. Ref.	Debit	Credit	Balance Debit	Balance Credit

Chapter 7, P 1. (Continued)

3. **Accounts receivable subsidiary ledger accounts opened**
5. **Transactions posted**

Accounts Receivable Subsidiary Ledger

A. Barrel

Date	Item	Post. Ref.	Debit	Credit	Balance

L. Lozocek

Date	Item	Post. Ref.	Debit	Credit	Balance

R. Woodman

Date	Item	Post. Ref.	Debit	Credit	Balance

Chapter 7, P 1. (Continued)

4. Accounts payable subsidiary ledger accounts opened
5. Transactions posted

Accounts Payable Subsidiary Ledger

Bayle Company

Date	Item	Post. Ref.	Debit	Credit	Balance

Centro Company

Date	Item	Post. Ref.	Debit	Credit	Balance

7. Schedules of accounts receivable and accounts payable prepared

Maher Company
Schedule of Accounts Receivable
May 31, 20xx

Maher Company
Schedule of Accounts Payable
May 31, 20xx

8. Relationship of subsidiary ledgers to controlling accounts explained

Chapter 7, P 2.

1. Transactions entered
2. Journals footed and crossfooted

Cash Receipts Journal

Page 1

Date	Account Debited/Credited	Post. Ref.	Debits			Credits		
			Cash	Sales Discounts	Other Accounts	Accounts Receivable	Sales	Other Accounts
Nov. 4	J. Walker		980	20		1,000		

Chapter 7, P 2. (Continued)

Cash Payments Journal

Page 1

Date	Ck. No.	Payee	Account Credited/Debited	Post. Ref.	Cash	Credits			Debits	
						Purchases Discounts	Other Accounts	Accounts Payable		Other Accounts
Nov. 1	782	R. Carello	Rent Expense		1,000					1,000

3. Source of total sales explained

Chapter 7, P 3.

1. Transactions entered in general journal and purchases journal

Date	Description	Post. Ref.	Debit	Credit

General Journal — Page 1

Chapter 7, P 3. (Continued)

2. Purchases journal footed and crossfooted

Purchases Journal Page 1

Date	Account Credited	Date of Invoice	Terms	Post. Ref.	Credit Accounts Payable	Debits Purchases	Debits Freight In	Debits Store Supplies	Debits Office Supplies	Other Accounts Account	Other Accounts Post. Ref.	Other Accounts Amount
July 2	Diego Fertilizer Company	7/2	n/30	✓	2,640	2,640						

Chapter 7, P 3. (Continued)

3. General ledger and accounts payable subsidiary ledger accounts opened and posted

General Ledger

Store Supplies — Account No. 116

Date	Item	Post. Ref.	Debit	Credit	Balance Debit	Balance Credit

Office Supplies — Account No. 117

Date	Item	Post. Ref.	Debit	Credit	Balance Debit	Balance Credit

Lawn Equipment — Account No. 142

Date	Item	Post. Ref.	Debit	Credit	Balance Debit	Balance Credit

Display Equipment — Account No. 144

Date	Item	Post. Ref.	Debit	Credit	Balance Debit	Balance Credit

Cleaning Equipment — Account No. 146

Date	Item	Post. Ref.	Debit	Credit	Balance Debit	Balance Credit

Accounts Payable — Account No. 211

Date	Item	Post. Ref.	Debit	Credit	Balance Debit	Balance Credit

Chapter 7, P 3. (Continued)

Purchases — Account No. 611

Date	Item	Post. Ref.	Debit	Credit	Balance Debit	Balance Credit

Purchases Returns and Allowances — Account No. 612

Date	Item	Post. Ref.	Debit	Credit	Balance Debit	Balance Credit

Freight In — Account No. 613

Date	Item	Post. Ref.	Debit	Credit	Balance Debit	Balance Credit

Accounts Payable Subsidiary Ledger

Brandon Lawn Equipment Company

Date	Item	Post. Ref.	Debit	Credit	Balance

Diego Fertilizer Company

Date	Item	Post. Ref.	Debit	Credit	Balance

Laronne Supply, Inc.

Date	Item	Post. Ref.	Debit	Credit	Balance

Whitman Company

Date	Item	Post. Ref.	Debit	Credit	Balance

Chapter 7, P 4.

1. Special-purpose journals and general journal prepared
5. Transactions entered in journals
6. Journals footed and crossfooted

\multicolumn{6}{c}{Sales Journal}	Page 1
Date	Account Debited	Invoice Number	Terms	Post. Ref.	Debit Accounts Receivable/ Credit Sales
May 9	Midtown Center	1001	5/10, n/30		1,564

Chapter 7, P 4. (Continued)

Purchases Journal Page 1

Date	Account Credited	Date of Invoice	Terms	Post. Ref.	Credit — Accounts Payable	Debits — Purchases	Debits — Freight In	Debits — Other Accounts — Account	Debits — Other Accounts — Post. Ref.	Debits — Other Accounts — Amount
May 4	Chassman Books, Inc.	5/3	5/10, n/60		15,680	15,680				

Cash Receipts Journal Page 1

Date	Account Debited/Credited	Post. Ref.	Debits — Cash	Debits — Sales Discounts	Debits — Other Accounts	Credits — Accounts Receivable	Credits — Sales	Credits — Other Accounts
May 1	Linda Berrill, Capital	311	42,000					42,000

Chapter 7, P 4. (Continued)

Cash Payments Journal

Page 1

Date	Ck. No.	Payee	Account Credited/Debited	Post. Ref.	Cash	Credits		Debits	
						Purchases Discounts	Other Accounts	Accounts Payable	Other Accounts
May 3	C001	Remax Rentals	Rent Expense	613	1,000				1,000

Chapter 7, P 4. (Continued)

General Journal — Page 1

Date	Description	Post. Ref.	Debit	Credit

Chapter 7, P 4. (Continued)

2. General ledger accounts opened
5. Transactions posted
6. End-of-month postings made

General Ledger

Cash   Account No. 111

Date	Item	Post. Ref.	Debit	Credit	Balance Debit	Balance Credit

Accounts Receivable   Account No. 112

Date	Item	Post. Ref.	Debit	Credit	Balance Debit	Balance Credit

Store Equipment   Account No. 141

Date	Item	Post. Ref.	Debit	Credit	Balance Debit	Balance Credit

Accounts Payable   Account No. 211

Date	Item	Post. Ref.	Debit	Credit	Balance Debit	Balance Credit

Notes Payable   Account No. 212

Date	Item	Post. Ref.	Debit	Credit	Balance Debit	Balance Credit

Chapter 7, P 4. (Continued)

Linda Berrill, Capital — Account No. 311

Date	Item	Post. Ref.	Debit	Credit	Balance Debit	Balance Credit

Sales — Account No. 411

Date	Item	Post. Ref.	Debit	Credit	Balance Debit	Balance Credit

Sales Discounts — Account No. 412

Date	Item	Post. Ref.	Debit	Credit	Balance Debit	Balance Credit

Sales Returns and Allowances — Account No. 413

Date	Item	Post. Ref.	Debit	Credit	Balance Debit	Balance Credit

Purchases — Account No. 511

Date	Item	Post. Ref.	Debit	Credit	Balance Debit	Balance Credit

Purchases Discounts — Account No. 512

Date	Item	Post. Ref.	Debit	Credit	Balance Debit	Balance Credit

Chapter 7, P 4. (Continued)

Purchases Returns and Allowances — Account No. 513

Date	Item	Post. Ref.	Debit	Credit	Balance Debit	Balance Credit

Freight In — Account No. 514

Date	Item	Post. Ref.	Debit	Credit	Balance Debit	Balance Credit

Sales Salaries Expense — Account No. 611

Date	Item	Post. Ref.	Debit	Credit	Balance Debit	Balance Credit

Advertising Expense — Account No. 612

Date	Item	Post. Ref.	Debit	Credit	Balance Debit	Balance Credit

Rent Expense — Account No. 613

Date	Item	Post. Ref.	Debit	Credit	Balance Debit	Balance Credit

Chapter 7, P 4. (Continued)

3. Accounts receivable subsidiary ledger accounts opened
5. Transactions posted

Accounts Receivable Subsidiary Ledger

Midtown Center

Date	Item	Post. Ref.	Debit	Credit	Balance

Steve Oahani

Date	Item	Post. Ref.	Debit	Credit	Balance

Missy Porter

Date	Item	Post. Ref.	Debit	Credit	Balance

Chapter 7, P 4. (Continued)

4. Accounts payable subsidiary ledger accounts opened
5. Transactions posted

Accounts Payable Subsidiary Ledger

Chassman Books, Inc.

Date	Item	Post. Ref.	Debit	Credit	Balance

Lakeside Books

Date	Item	Post. Ref.	Debit	Credit	Balance

Menden Shippers

Date	Item	Post. Ref.	Debit	Credit	Balance

Perspectives Publishing Company

Date	Item	Post. Ref.	Debit	Credit	Balance

Chapter 7, P 4. (Continued)

7. Trial balance and schedules of accounts receivable and accounts payable prepared

Ye Olde Book Store
Trial Balance
May 31, 20xx

Ye Olde Book Store
Schedule of Accounts Receivable
May 31, 20xx

Ye Olde Book Store
Schedule of Accounts Payable
May 31, 20xx

Chapter 7, P 5.

1. Special-purpose journals and general journal prepared
5. Transactions entered in journals
6. Journals footed and crossfooted

				Sales Journal	Page 1
Date	Account Debited	Invoice Number	Post. Ref.	Amount (Debit Accounts Receivable/ Credit Sales)	

Chapter 7, P 5. (Continued)

Purchases Journal

Page 1

Date	Account Credited	Date of Invoice	Terms	Post. Ref.	Credit	Debits		Other Accounts		
					Accounts Payable	Purchases	Freight In	Account	Post. Ref.	Amount

Chapter 7, P 5. (Continued)

Cash Receipts Journal
Page 1

Date	Account Debited/Credited	Post. Ref.	Debits			Credits	
			Cash	Sales Discounts	Other Accounts	Accounts Receivable	Sales	Other Accounts

Cash Payments Journal
Page 1

Date	Ck. No.	Payee	Account Credited/Debited	Post. Ref.	Credits			Debits	
					Cash	Purchases Discounts	Other Accounts	Accounts Payable	Other Accounts

Chapter 7, P 5. (Continued)

Date	Description	Post. Ref.	Debit	Credit

General Journal — Page 1

Chapter 7, P 5. (Continued)

2. General ledger accounts opened
5. Transactions posted
6. End-of-month postings made

General Ledger

Cash — 111

Date		Post. Ref.	Debit	Credit	Balance Debit	Balance Credit

Accounts Receivable — 112

Date		Post. Ref.	Debit	Credit	Balance Debit	Balance Credit

Office Equipment — 141

Date		Post. Ref.	Debit	Credit	Balance Debit	Balance Credit

Accounts Payable — 211

Date		Post. Ref.	Debit	Credit	Balance Debit	Balance Credit

Sales — 411

Date		Post. Ref.	Debit	Credit	Balance Debit	Balance Credit

Chapter 7, P 5. (Continued)

Sales Discounts 412

Date		Post. Ref.	Debit	Credit	Balance Debit	Balance Credit

Sales Returns and Allowances 413

Date		Post. Ref.	Debit	Credit	Balance Debit	Balance Credit

Purchases 511

Date		Post. Ref.	Debit	Credit	Balance Debit	Balance Credit

Purchases Discounts 512

Date		Post. Ref.	Debit	Credit	Balance Debit	Balance Credit

Purchases Returns and Allowances 513

Date		Post. Ref.	Debit	Credit	Balance Debit	Balance Credit

Freight In 514

Date		Post. Ref.	Debit	Credit	Balance Debit	Balance Credit

Chapter 7, P 5. (Continued)

Sales Salaries Expense 521

Date		Post. Ref.	Debit	Credit	Balance Debit	Balance Credit

Advertising Expense 522

Date		Post. Ref.	Debit	Credit	Balance Debit	Balance Credit

Rent Expense 531

Date		Post. Ref.	Debit	Credit	Balance Debit	Balance Credit

Repairs Expense 532

Date		Post. Ref.	Debit	Credit	Balance Debit	Balance Credit

Chapter 7, P 5. (Continued)

3. Accounts receivable subsidiary ledger accounts opened
5. Transactions posted

Accounts Receivable Subsidiary Ledger

H. Blake

Date		Post. Ref.	Debit	Credit	Balance

K. Hanama

Date		Post. Ref.	Debit	Credit	Balance

J. Koppel

Date		Post. Ref.	Debit	Credit	Balance

Chapter 7, P 5. (Continued)

4. Accounts payable subsidiary ledger accounts opened
5. Transactions posted

Accounts Payable Subsidiary Ledger

LaRocke Manufacturing

Date		Post. Ref.	Debit	Credit	Balance

Tate Company

Date		Post. Ref.	Debit	Credit	Balance

Winters Company

Date		Post. Ref.	Debit	Credit	Balance

WRRT

Date		Post. Ref.	Debit	Credit	Balance

Chapter 7, P 5. (Continued)

7. Trial balance and schedules of accounts receivable and accounts payable prepared

Fahner Refrigeration Company
Trial Balance
October 31, 20xx

Fahner Refrigeration Company
Schedule of Accounts Receivable
October 31, 20xx

Fahner Refrigeration Company
Schedule of Accounts Payable
October 31, 20xx

Chapter 7, P 6.

1. Special-purpose journals and general journal prepared
5. Transactions entered in journals
6. Journals footed and crossfooted

Sales Journal						Page 1
Date	Account Debited	Invoice Number	Terms	Post. Ref.	Debit Accounts Receivable/ Credit Sales	

Chapter 7, P 6. (Continued)

Purchases Journal

Page 1

Date	Account Credited	Date of Invoice	Terms	Post. Ref.	Debit Purchases/ Credit Accounts Payable

Cash Receipts Journal

Page 1

Date	Account Debited/Credited	Post. Ref.	Debits			Credits		
			Cash	Sales Discounts	Other Accounts	Accounts Receivable	Sales	Other Accounts

Cash Payments Journal

Page 1

Date	Ck. No.	Payee	Account Credited/Debited	Post. Ref.	Credits			Debits		
					Cash	Purchases Discounts	Other Accounts	Accounts Payable	Other Accounts	

Chapter 7, P 6. (Continued)

General Journal — Page 1

Date	Description	Post. Ref.	Debit	Credit

2. General ledger accounts opened
5. Transactions posted
6. End-of-month postings made

General Ledger

Accounts Receivable — Account No. 112

Date	Item	Post. Ref.	Debit	Credit	Balance Debit	Balance Credit

Accounts Payable — Account No. 211

Date	Item	Post. Ref.	Debit	Credit	Balance Debit	Balance Credit

Chapter 7, P 6. (Continued)

3. Accounts receivable subsidiary ledger accounts opened
5. Transactions posted

Accounts Receivable Subsidiary Ledger

M. Abdul

Date	Item	Post. Ref.	Debit	Credit	Balance

T. Bacon

Date	Item	Post. Ref.	Debit	Credit	Balance

R. Banks

Date	Item	Post. Ref.	Debit	Credit	Balance

Chapter 7, P 6. (Continued)

4. Accounts payable subsidiary ledger accounts opened
5. Transactions posted

Accounts Payable Subsidiary Ledger

Shalkor Inc.

Date	Item	Post. Ref.	Debit	Credit	Balance

Ventman Company

Date	Item	Post. Ref.	Debit	Credit	Balance

7. Schedules of accounts receivable and accounts payable prepared

Simons Company
Schedule of Accounts Receivable
June 30, 20xx

Simons Company
Schedule of Accounts Payable
June 30, 20xx

8. Relationship of subsidiary ledgers to controlling accounts explained

Chapter 7, P 7.

1. Transactions entered in cash receipts and cash payments journals
2. Journals footed and crossfooted

Cash Receipts Journal

Date	Account Debited/Credited	Post. Ref.	Debits			Credits		
			Cash	Sales Discounts	Other Accounts	Accounts Receivable	Sales	Other Accounts
Oct. 1	Equipment/Michael O'Malley, Capital		50,000		24,000			74,000

Cash Payments Journal

Date	Ck. No.	Payee	Account Credited/Debited	Post. Ref.	Credits			Debits		
					Cash	Purchases Discounts	Other Accounts	Accounts Payable	Other Accounts	
Oct. 2	75	Bellamy Agency	Rent Expense		600				600	

Chapter 7, P 7. (Continued)

3. **Source of total sales explained**

Chapter 7, P 8.

1. Special-purpose journals and general journal prepared
5. Transactions entered in journals
6. Journals footed and crossfooted

Sales Journal						Page 1
Date	Account Debited	Invoice Number	Terms	Post. Ref.	Debit Accounts Receivable/ Credit Sales	

Chapter 7, P 8. (Continued)

Purchases Journal
Page 1

Date	Account Credited	Date of Invoice	Terms	Post. Ref.	Credit Accounts Payable	Debits Purchases	Debits Freight In	Debits Other Accounts Account	Debits Other Accounts Post. Ref.	Debits Other Accounts Amount

Chapter 7, P 8. (Continued)

Cash Receipts Journal   Page 1

Date	Account Debited/Credited	Post. Ref.	Debits			Credits		
			Cash	Sales Discounts	Other Accounts	Accounts Receivable	Sales	Other Accounts

Cash Payments Journal   Page 1

Date	Ck. No.	Payee	Account Credited/Debited	Post. Ref.	Credits			Debits	
					Cash	Purchases Discounts	Other Accounts	Accounts Payable	Other Accounts

Chapter 7, P 8. (Continued)

General Journal   Page 1

Date	Description	Post. Ref.	Debit	Credit

2. General ledger accounts opened
5. Transactions posted
6. End-of-month postings made

General Ledger

Cash   Account No. 111

Date	Item	Post. Ref.	Debit	Credit	Balance Debit	Balance Credit

Accounts Receivable   Account No. 112

Date	Item	Post. Ref.	Debit	Credit	Balance Debit	Balance Credit

Store Equipment   Account No. 141

Date	Item	Post. Ref.	Debit	Credit	Balance Debit	Balance Credit

Accounts Payable   Account No. 211

Date	Item	Post. Ref.	Debit	Credit	Balance Debit	Balance Credit

Chapter 7, P. 8. (Continued)

Notes Payable — Account No. 212

Date	Item	Post. Ref.	Debit	Credit	Balance Debit	Balance Credit

Garrett Stackpole, Capital — Account No. 311

Date	Item	Post. Ref.	Debit	Credit	Balance Debit	Balance Credit

Sales — Account No. 411

Date	Item	Post. Ref.	Debit	Credit	Balance Debit	Balance Credit

Sales Discounts — Account No. 412

Date	Item	Post. Ref.	Debit	Credit	Balance Debit	Balance Credit

Sales Returns and Allowances — Account No. 413

Date	Item	Post. Ref.	Debit	Credit	Balance Debit	Balance Credit

Purchases — Account No. 511

Date	Item	Post. Ref.	Debit	Credit	Balance Debit	Balance Credit

Purchases Discounts — Account No. 512

Date	Item	Post. Ref.	Debit	Credit	Balance Debit	Balance Credit

Purchases Returns and Allowances — Account No. 513

Date	Item	Post. Ref.	Debit	Credit	Balance Debit	Balance Credit

Chapter 7, P 8. (Continued)

Freight In   Account No. 514

Date	Item	Post. Ref.	Debit	Credit	Balance Debit	Balance Credit

Sales Salaries Expense   Account No. 611

Date	Item	Post. Ref.	Debit	Credit	Balance Debit	Balance Credit

Advertising Expense   Account No. 612

Date	Item	Post. Ref.	Debit	Credit	Balance Debit	Balance Credit

Rent Expense   Account No. 613

Date	Item	Post. Ref.	Debit	Credit	Balance Debit	Balance Credit

Chapter 7, P 8. (Continued)

3. Accounts receivable subsidiary ledger accounts opened
5. Transactions posted

Accounts Receivable Subsidiary Ledger

Avon Old Farms School

Date	Item	Post. Ref.	Debit	Credit	Balance

Missy Cavanaugh

Date	Item	Post. Ref.	Debit	Credit	Balance

Alicia Menotte

Date	Item	Post. Ref.	Debit	Credit	Balance

Chapter 7, P 8. (Continued)

4. Accounts payable subsidiary ledger accounts opened
5. Transactions posted

Accounts Payable Subsidiary Ledger

Cronos Company

Date	Item	Post. Ref.	Debit	Credit	Balance

Gallagher Company

Date	Item	Post. Ref.	Debit	Credit	Balance

Sentinel-Gazette

Date	Item	Post. Ref.	Debit	Credit	Balance

Seagal Company

Date	Item	Post. Ref.	Debit	Credit	Balance

Chapter 7, P 8. (Continued)

7. Trial balance and schedules of accounts receivable and accounts payable prepared

Stackpole's Men's Wear
Trial Balance
May 31, 20xx

Stackpole's Men's Wear
Schedule of Accounts Receivable
May 31, 20xx

Stackpole's Men's Wear
Schedule of Accounts Payable
May 31, 20xx

Chapter 7, SD 1.

Memorandum

Date:
To:
From:
Re:

(continued)

Chapter 7, SD 1. (Continued)

Chapter 7, SD 2.

Chapter 7, SD 3.

Chapter 7, FRA 1.

1.

2.

(continued)

Chapter 7, FRA 1. (Continued)

3.

Chapter 7, FRA 2.

Chapter 8, SE 1.

Chapter 8, SE 2.

1.		4.	
2.		5.	
3.			

Chapter 8, SE 3.

1.		3.	
2.		4.	

Chapter 8, SE 4.

1.		5.	
2.		6.	
3.		7.	
4.			

Chapter 8, SE 5.

	Where Prepared	Where Sent
1.		
2.		
3.		
4.		
5.		

Chapter 8, SE 6.

1.		3.	
2.		4.	

Chapter 8, SE 7.

Balance per bank, June 30	$2,586.58
Balance per books, June 30	$1,308.87

Chapter 8, SE 8.

20xx				

Chapter 8, SE 9.

1.		3.	
2.		4.	

Chapter 8, SE 10.

The proper order of the actions is:

Chapter 8, E 1.

1.

2.

3.

4.

Chapter 8, E 2.

1.
2.
3.
4.
5.

Chapter 8, E 3.

Chapter 8, E 4.

Chapter 8, E 5.

1.
2.
3.
4.

Chapter 8, E 6.

Chapter 8, E 7.

a.
b.
c.
d.

Chapter 8, E 8.

Chapter 8, E 9.

Chapter 8, E 10.

20xx				

Chapter 8, P 1.

1. **Bank reconciliation prepared**

Costa Company Bank Reconciliation April 30, 20xx		
Balance per bank, April 30, 20xx		
Adjusted bank balance, April 30, 20xx		
Balance per books, April 30, 20xx		
Adjusted book balance, April 30, 20xx		

Chapter 8, P 1. (Continued)

2. Entries prepared

20xx				

3. Cash balance identified

The adjusted balance of _____ should appear on the balance sheet.

Chapter 8, P 2.

1. Bank reconciliation prepared

Sultani Company
Bank Reconciliation
November 30, 20xx

Balance per bank, November 30, 20xx		$141,717.08
Balance per books, November 30, 20xx		$113,675.28

Chapter 8, P 2. (Continued)

2. Entries prepared

20xx				

3. Correct cash balance identified

The adjusted balance of _____ should appear on the balance sheet.

4. Control activity identified and discussed

Chapter 8, P 3.

20xx				

Chapter 8, P 4.

Authorization

Recording transactions

Documents and records

Physical controls

Periodic independent verification

Separation of duties

Sound personnel policies

Chapter 8, P 5.

1. Voucher register, check register, and journal entries prepared

Voucher Register

Page 18

	Voucher No.	Payee	Payment Date	Check No.	Credit Vouchers Payable	Purchases	Debits Freight In	Store Supplies	Office Supplies	Sales Salaries Expense	Office Salaries Expense	Other Accounts Name	Amount
Date													
20xx													
July 1	205	Petty Cash Cashier	7/2	330	500							Petty Cash	500

Note: The expense columns Maintenance, Selling; Maintenance, Office; and Utilities have no entries and so have been deleted.

Chapter 8, P 5. (Continued)

Check Register — Page 12

Date	Check No.	Payee	Voucher No.	Debit Vouchers Payable	Credits Purchases Discounts	Cash
20xx						
July 2	330	Petty Cash Cashier	205	500		500

General Journal — Page 10

Date	Description	Post. Ref.	Debit	Credit
20xx				

Chapter 8, P 5. (Continued)

2. Vouchers Payable account prepared

Vouchers Payable — Account No. 211

Date	Item	Post. Ref.	Debit	Credit	Balance Debit	Balance Credit
20xx						

3. Schedule of unpaid vouchers prepared

Second Star Toy Shop
Schedule of Unpaid Vouchers
July 31, 20xx

Payee	Voucher No.	Amount

Chapter 8, P 6.

Authorization

Recording transactions

Documents and records

Physical controls

Periodic independent verification

Separation of duties

Sound personnel policies

Chapter 8, P 7.

1. Bank reconciliation prepared

Manuel Suarez Company Bank Reconciliation October 31, 20xx		
Balance per bank, October 31, 20xx		$26,175.73
Balance per books, October 31, 20xx		$21,327.08

Chapter 8, P 7. (Continued)

2. Entries prepared

20xx Oct. 31				

3. Correct cash balance identified

The adjusted balance of _____ should appear on the balance sheet.

4. Control activity identified and discussed

Chapter 8, P 8.

20xx				

Chapter 8, SD 1.

The control activities that were likely violated in this case were as follows:

a.

b.

c.

d.

Chapter 8, SD 2.

Chapter 8, SD 2. (Continued)

Chapter 8, SD 3.

Chapter 8, SD 5.

Memorandum

To:
From:
Date:
Re:

Chapter 8, FRA 1.

Chapter 8, FRA 2.

Chapter 9, SE 1.

1.
2.
3.
4.

Chapter 9, SE 2.

Quick Ratio	=	Short-Term Financial Assets / Current Liabilities	
	=		
	=		
Receivable Turnover	=		
	=		
	=		
Average Days' Sales Uncollected	=		
	=		

Chapter 9, SE 3.

Chapter 9, SE 4.

Chapter 9, SE 5.

20x1					

Chapter 9, SE 6.

Chapter 9, SE 7.

(a)

(b)

Chapter 9, SE 8.

Chapter 9, SE 9.

Chapter 9, E 1.

1.	
2.	
3.	
4.	
5.	
6.	
7.	
8.	

Chapter 9, E 2.

Quick Ratio	=		
	=		
	=		
Receivable Turnover	=		
	=		
	=		
Average Days' Sales Uncollected	=		
	=		

Chapter 9, E 3.

Chapter 9, E 4.

20x1				

Chapter 9, E 5.

Jan.	6				
		Security	Cost	Market Value	Gain/(Loss)
		General Mills (shares)			
		Delta (shares)			
		Totals			

Chapter 9, E 6.

The balance of Allowance for Uncollectible Accounts after this adjustment:

Chapter 9, E 7.

a.

b.

The balance of Allowance for Uncollectible Accounts after each of these adjustments is:

Chapter 9, E 8.

T accounts prepared to determine ending balances:

Accounts Receivable

Allowance for Uncollectible Accounts

a. Percentage of net sales method applied

Adjusting entry:

Chapter 9, E 8. (Continued)

Balance sheet presentation:

Allowance for Uncollectible Accounts

b. Aging of accounts receivable method applied

Adjusting entry:

Balance sheet presentation:

Allowance for Uncollectible Accounts

Chapter 9, E 9.

a.

The balance of Allowance for Uncollectible Accounts after this adjustment:

b.

The balance of Allowance for Uncollectible Accounts after this adjustment:

Chapter 9, E 10.

Entries for uncollectible accounts prepared

a. Percentage of net sales method:

The resulting balance of Allowance for Uncollectible Accounts:

If the beginning balance of Allowance for Uncollectible Accounts had been a credit, the entry would have been:

The resulting balance of would have been:

b. Accounts receivable aging method:

The resulting balance of Allowance for Uncollectible Accounts:

If the beginning balance of Allowance for Uncollectible Accounts had been a credit, the entry would have been:

The resulting balance of would have been:

Why do the methods result in different balances?

Chapter 9, E 11.

20x4				

Chapter 9, E 12.

a.	$22,800	x	10	/	100	x	90	/	360	=	
b.											
c.											
d.											
e.											

Chapter 9, E 13.

Chapter 9, E 14.

Chapter 9, E 15.

Chapter 9, P 1.

1. Entries prepared

20x1

Chapter 9, P 1. (Continued)

20x1				

Chapter 9, P 1. (Continued)

Chapter 9, P 1. (Continued)

2. Balance sheet presentation shown

Chapter 9, P 2.

1. T accounts prepared and data entered

Accounts Receivable

Allowance for Uncollectible Accounts

2. Uncollectible Accounts Expense and ending balance of Allowance for Uncollectible Accounts determined

a. Percentage of net sales method:

Uncollectible Accounts Expense =
=
=

Allowance for Uncollectible Accounts =
=

Accounts Receivable, Net =
=

b. Accounts receivable aging method:

Uncollectible Accounts Expense =
=

Allowance for Uncollectible Accounts =

Accounts Receivable, Net =
=

Chapter 9, P 2. (Continued)

3. Receivable turnover and average days' sales uncollected calculated

Receivable Turnover =

=

Average Days' Sales Uncollected =

4. Difference in methods and rationales discussed

Chapter 9, P 3.

1. Aging analysis completed

Avioni Fashions Store
Aging Analysis of Accounts Receivable
January 31, 20x2

Customer Account	Total	Not Yet Due	1–30 Days Past Due	31–60 Days Past Due	61–90 Days Past Due	Over 90 Days Past Due
Balance Forward						

2. End-of-year balances computed

Accounts Receivable		
Beginning balance		$ 446,341
Allowance for Uncollectible Accounts		

Chapter 9, P 3. (Continued)

3. Analysis of estimated uncollectible accounts prepared

Avioni Fashions Store
Estimated Uncollectible Accounts
January 31, 20x2

	Amount	Percentage Considered Uncollectible	Allowance for Uncollectible Accounts
Not yet due	$452,636	2	$ 9,052.72

4. Entry for uncollectible accounts expense prepared in journal form

20x2				

Chapter 9, P 4.

20xx

Chapter 9, P 4. (Continued)

20xx				

Chapter 9, P 4. (Continued)

Chapter 9, P 5.

1. Entries prepared

20x1				

Chapter 9, P 5. (Continued)

20x1				

Chapter 9, P 5. (Continued)

2. Balance sheet presentation shown

Chapter 9, P 6.

1. T accounts prepared and data entered

Accounts Receivable

Allowance for Uncollectible Accounts

2. Uncollectible Accounts Expense and ending balance of Allowance for Uncollectible Accounts determined

a. Percentage of net sales method:

Uncollectible Accounts Expense	=	
	=	
	=	
Allowance for Uncollectible Accounts	=	
	=	
Accounts Receivable, Net	=	
	=	

b. Accounts receivable aging method:

Uncollectible Accounts Expense	=	
	=	
Allowance for Uncollectible Accounts	=	
Accounts Receivable, Net	=	
	=	

Chapter 9, P 6. (Continued)

3. Receivable turnover and average days' sales uncollected calculated

Receivable Turnover =

=

Average Days' Sales Uncollected =

4. Difference in methods and rationales discussed

Chapter 9, P 7.

1. Aging analysis completed

Pinero Company
Aging Analysis of Accounts Receivable
December 31, 20xx

Customer Account	Total	Not Yet Due	1–30 Days Past Due	31–60 Days Past Due	61–90 Days Past Due	Over 90 Days Past Due
Balance Forward	$89,640	$49,030	$24,110	$9,210	$3,990	$3,300

2. End-of-year balances computed

Accounts Receivable

Allowance for Uncollectible Accounts

Chapter 9, P 7. (Continued)

3. Analysis of estimated uncollectible accounts prepared

Pinero Company
Estimated Uncollectible Accounts
December 31, 20xx

	Amount	Percentage Considered Uncollectible	Allowance for Uncollectible Accounts
Not yet due	$52,645	2	$1,052.90

4. Entry for uncollectible accounts expense prepared in journal form

Dec.	31			

Chapter 9, P 8.					
Jan.	10				
Chapter 9, P 8.					

Chapter 9, P 8. (Continued)

Chapter 9, SD 1.

Memorandum

Date:
To:
From:
Re:

Chapter 9, SD 2.

Chapter 9, SD 3.

Chapter 9, SD 6.

1. Investment transactions recorded

Chapter 9, SD 6. (Continued)

2. Balance sheet presentation on June 30 shown

3. Allowance account discussed

4. Strategy assessed

Chapter 9, FRA 1.

Chapter 9, FRA 2.

1. Ratios computed (dollar amounts in thousands)

	2001	2000	1999
Ratio of Uncollectible Accounts Expense			
To Net Sales	_____ =	_____ =	_____ =
To Accounts Receivable	_____ =	_____ =	_____ =
Ratio of Allowance for Uncollectible Accounts			
To Accounts Receivable	_____ =	_____ =	_____ =

Chapter 9, FRA 2. (Continued)

2. **Ratios calculated** (dollar amounts in thousands)

Receivable Turnover	=	

(Note: The net accounts receivable need to be calculated for 2001, 2000, and 1999.)

2001	=	
	=	
2000	=	
	=	
1999	=	
	=	
Average Days' Sales Uncollected	=	
2001	=	
2000	=	
1999	=	

Chapter 9, FRA 2. (Continued)

3. Interpretation of ratios

Chapter 9, FRA 3.

Chapter 9, FRA 4.

1. Cash and cash equivalents discussed

2. Allowance for Uncollectible Accounts discussed

Chapter 9, FRA 4. (Continued)

3. Quick ratios computed and discussed (in thousands)

	Quick Ratio	=	
	2002:		
		=	
	2001:		
		=	

Chapter 9, FRA 4. (Continued)

4. **Receivable ratios computed and discussed** (in thousands)

Receivable Turnover	=	
2001:	=	
2002:	=	

Average Days' Sales Uncollected	=	
2001:		
2002:		

Chapter 9, FRA 5.

1. Quick ratios calculated and discussed (in thousands)

Toys "R" Us quick ratio (from FRA 4):

    2002:

    2001:

Walgreens quick ratio:

    Quick Ratio =

    2001:

    =

    2002:

    =

2. Seasonality discussed

Chapter 10, SE 1.

1.   3.
2.   4.

Chapter 10, SE 2.

Inventory Turnover =

=

=

Average Days' Inventory on Hand =

=

Chapter 10, SE 3.

Specific identification method:

Chapter 10, SE 4.

Average-cost method—periodic inventory system:

Chapter 10, SE 5.

FIFO method—periodic inventory system:

Chapter 10, SE 6.

LIFO method—periodic inventory system:

Chapter 10, SE 7.

Average-cost method—perpetual inventory system:

				Cost per Unit	Amount
Aug.	1	Inventory		80	$10.00	$ 800

Cost of goods sold

Chapter 10, SE 8.

FIFO method—perpetual inventory system:

			Units	Cost per Unit		
Aug.	1	Inventory	80	$10		$ 800
Cost of goods sold						

Chapter 10, SE 9.

LIFO method—perpetual inventory system:

			Units	Cost per Unit		
Aug.	1	Inventory	80	$10		$ 800
Cost of goods sold						

Chapter 10, SE 10.

	Specific Identification Method	Periodic Inventory System			Perpetual Inventory System		
		Average-Cost Method	FIFO Method	LIFO Method	Average-Cost Method	FIFO Method	LIFO Method
Ending inventory							
Cost of goods sold							

Discussion:

Chapter 10, SE 11.

Item	Quantity	Cost per Unit	Market per Unit	Cost	Market	Item-by-Item
Short sleeve	280	$24	$20			
Long sleeve	190	28	29			
Extra-long sleeve	80	34	35			

Lower of cost or market on an item-by-item basis:

Lower of cost or market on a major category basis:

Chapter 10, E 1.

1.
2.
3.
4.
5.
6.

Chapter 10, E 2.

Inventory Turnover =

20x3: =

=

20x2: =

=

Average Days' Inventory on Hand =

20x3: =

20x2: =

Chapter 10, E 3.

1. Inventory costs assigned by the specific identification method

June	15	Purchase,		cases	@		

Cost of goods sold

Ending inventory

2. Inventory costs assigned by the average-cost method

Average unit cost:

Cost of goods available for sale	$36,550

3. Inventory costs assigned by the FIFO method

Cost of goods sold		

4. Inventory costs assigned by the LIFO method

Cost of goods sold		

(continued)

Chapter 10, E 3. (Continued)

Conclusions:

Chapter 10, E 4.

1. Cost of goods sold computed by FIFO method

	Year 1	Year 2	Year 3

2. Cost of goods sold computed by LIFO method

	Year 1	Year 2	Year 3

Conclusions:

Chapter 10, E 5.

Sales		units x	$60		
		units x			
		units x			
		units x			
		units x			
		units			
Beginning inventory		units x			
Purchases		units x			
		units x			
		units x			
Cost of goods available for sale		units			

Periodic inventory system—average-cost method:

Sales					$165,000

Periodic inventory system—FIFO method:

Chapter 10, E 5. (Continued)

Periodic inventory system—LIFO method:

Differences in gross margin explained:

Chapter 10, E 6.

Perpetual inventory system—average-cost method

Date			Units	Cost	Amount
June	1	Inventory			

Sales		
Cost of goods sold		
Gross margin		

Computations:

	Sales	Cost of Goods Sold	
Total			

Chapter 10, E 6. (Continued)

Perpetual inventory system—FIFO method

Date			Units	Cost	Amount
June	1	Inventory			

Sales	
Cost of goods sold	
Gross margin	

Computations:

	Sales	Cost of Goods Sold	
Total			

Chapter 10, E 6. (Continued)

Perpetual inventory system—LIFO method

Date			Units	Cost	Amount
June	1	Inventory			

Chapter 10, E 6. (Continued)

Sales		
Cost of goods sold		
Gross margin		

Computations:

	Sales	Cost of Goods Sold
Total		

The difference in gross margin explained:

Chapter 10, E 7.

Goods available for sale and ending inventory in units

	Units	Cost	Total
Beginning inventory	100	$ 2	
Ending inventory in units			

Chapter 10, E 7. (Continued)

1. Periodic inventory system

a. Specific identification method:

Sales

b. Average-cost method:

c. FIFO method:

Chapter 10, E 7. (Continued)

d.	LIFO method:		
	Sales		$4,000

2. Perpetual inventory system

a. Average-cost method:

Sales	
Cost of goods sold	
Gross margin	

	Units	Cost	Amount	
Beginning inventory				
Purchase 1				
Balance				
Sale 1				
Balance				
Purchase 2				
Balance				
Purchase 3				
Balance				
Purchase 4				
Balance				
Sale 2				
Balance				
Purchase 5				
Ending inventory				

Chapter 10, E 7. (Continued)

b. FIFO method:

　　　Ending inventory =

c. LIFO method:

　　　Ending inventory =

Chapter 10, E 8.

	FIFO Method	LIFO Method
Sales		
Net income		

Comments:

Chapter 10, E 8. (Continued)

If a year-end purchase of 10,000 cases at $30 per case is made, the following will result:

	FIFO Method	LIFO Method
Sales		
Net income		

Comments:

Chapter 10, E 9.

1.		6.	
2.		7.	
3.		8.	
4.		9.	
5.		10.	

Chapter 10, E 10.

	20x5	20x4

Effect of error:

Chapter 10, E 11.

1. Lower-of-cost-or-market value computed, using the item-by-item method

	Quantity	Per Unit Cost	Per Unit Market	Lower of Cost or Market
Category I				
Item aa	200	$ 2.00	$ 1.80	
Item bb	240	4.00	4.40	
Item cc	400	8.00	7.50	
Category II				
Item dd	300	12.00	13.00	
Item ee	400	18.00	18.20	
Inventory at the lower of cost or market				

2. Lower-of-cost-or-market value computed, using the major category method

	Quantity	Per Unit Cost	Per Unit Market	Total Cost	Total Market	Lower of Cost or Market
Category I						
Item aa	200	$ 2.00	$ 1.80			
Item bb	240	4.00	4.40			
Item cc	400	8.00	7.50			
Totals						
Category II						
Item dd	300	12.00	13.00			
Item ee	400	18.00	18.20			
Totals						
Inventory at the lower of cost or market						

Chapter 10, E 12.

1. Ending inventory estimated by retail method

	Cost	Retail
Beginning inventory	$ 80,000	$120,000

2. Loss estimated

Chapter 10, E 13.

Chapter 10, P 1.

1. Schedule of cost of goods available for sale prepared

	Units	Price	Total Cost
Beginning inventory			
Purchases			
Cost of goods available for sale			

2. Income before income taxes computed

a. Average-cost method:

Chapter 10, P 1. (Continued)

b. FIFO method:

c. LIFO method:

Chapter 10, P 1. (Continued)

3. Ratios computed

	Average-Cost	FIFO	LIFO
Cost of goods sold			
Average inventory			
Inventory turnover			
Average days' inventory on hand			

Conclusion:

Chapter 10, P 2.

1. Periodic inventory system—average-cost method

	Units	Unit Price	Amount
March 1 beginning inventory	60	$49.00	
March 31 ending inventory			
Cost of goods sold for March			

April 1 beginning inventory						
	Units	Unit Price	Amount			
Purchases						
April 4						
April 30 ending inventory						
Cost of goods sold for April						

Chapter 10, P 2. (Continued)

2. Periodic inventory system—FIFO method

	Units	Unit Price	Amount
March 1 beginning inventory	60	$49	
April 1 beginning inventory			

	Units	Unit Price	Amount			
Purchases						
April 4						
April 30 ending inventory						
Cost of goods sold for April						

Chapter 10, P 2. (Continued)

3. Periodic inventory system—LIFO method

	Units	Unit Price	Amount
March 1 beginning inventory	60	$49	
March 31 ending inventory			
Cost of goods sold for March			

April 1 beginning inventory							
	Units	Unit Price	Amount				
Purchases							
April 4							
April 30 ending inventory							
Cost of goods sold for April							

Chapter 10, P 2. (Continued)

4. Effects on cash flows discussed

Chapter 10, P 3.

1. Perpetual inventory system—average-cost method

Date			Units	Cost*	Amount*
Mar.	1	Beginning inventory	60	$49.00	

*Rounded.

Cost of goods sold for March:

Cost of goods sold for April:

Chapter 10, P 3. (Continued)

2. Perpetual inventory system—FIFO method

Date			Units	Cost	Amount
Mar.	1	Beginning inventory	60	$49	

Cost of goods sold for March:

Cost of goods sold for April:

Chapter 10, P 3. (Continued)

3. Perpetual inventory system—LIFO method

Date			Units	Cost	Amount
Mar.	1	Beginning inventory	60	$49	

Cost of goods sold for March:

Cost of goods sold for April:

Chapter 10, P 4.

		Cost	Retail
1.	Beginning inventory		
	Estimated ending inventory at retail		
	Ratio of cost to retail		
	Estimated cost of ending inventory		
2.	October 31 physical inventory		
3.	Estimated inventory shortage at cost and retail		

Chapter 10, P 5.

Sabatino Sisters
Schedule to Estimate Inventory Destroyed
April 22, 20x2

Beginning inventory at cost		$ 727,400
Estimated loss of inventory in fire		

Chapter 10, P 6.

1. Schedule of cost of goods available for sale prepared

	Units	Price	Total Cost
Beginning inventory			

2. Income before income taxes computed

a. Average-cost method:

Chapter 10, P 6. (Continued)

b. FIFO method:

c. LIFO method:

Chapter 10, P 6. (Continued)

3. Ratios computed

	Average-Cost	FIFO	LIFO
Cost of goods sold			
Average inventory			
Inventory turnover			
Average days' inventory on hand			

Conclusion:

Chapter 10, P 7.

1. Periodic inventory system—average-cost method

	Units	Unit Price*	Amount
April 1 beginning inventory	50	$102.00	
Cost of goods sold for April			
May 1 beginning inventory			

	Units	Unit Price	Amount			
Purchases						
May 2						
Cost of goods sold for May						

*Rounded.

Chapter 10, P 7. (Continued)

2. Periodic inventory system—FIFO method

	Units	Unit Price	Amount
April 1 beginning inventory	50	$102	
Cost of goods sold for April			

May 1 beginning inventory

	Units	Unit Price	Amount	Units	Unit Price	Amount
Purchases						
May 2						
Cost of goods sold for May						

Chapter 10, P 7. (Continued)

3. Periodic inventory system—LIFO method

	Units	Unit Price	Amount
April 1 beginning inventory	50	$102	
Cost of goods sold for April			
May 1 beginning inventory			

	Units	Unit Price	Amount				
Purchases							
May 2							
Cost of goods sold for May							

Chapter 10, P 7. (Continued)

4. **Effects on cash flows discussed**

Chapter 10, P 8.

1. **Perpetual inventory system—average-cost method**

Date		Units	Cost*	Amount*
Apr.	1 Beginning inventory	50	$102.00	

*Rounded.

Cost of goods sold for April:

Cost of goods sold for May:

Chapter 10, P 8. (Continued)

2. Perpetual inventory system—FIFO method

Date			Units	Cost	Amount
Apr.	1	Beginning inventory	50	$102	

Cost of goods sold for April:

Cost of goods sold for May:

Chapter 10, P 8. (Continued)

3. Perpetual inventory system—LIFO method

Date		Units	Cost	Amount
Apr. 1	Beginning inventory	50	$102	

Chapter 10, P 8. (Continued)

Cost of goods sold for April:

Cost of goods sold for May:

Chapter 10, SD 1.

Chapter 10, SD 2.

Chapter 10, SD 3.

Chapter 10, SD 4.

Chapter 10, SD 6.

FIFO and LIFO methods with purchase compared

	FIFO Method	LIFO Method

Chapter 10, SD 6. (Continued)

Comparison of cash outcomes and recommendation of inventory system

	Memorandum			
Date:	Today's Date			
To:	Management			
From:	Student's Name			
Re:	Inventory Method and Purchase Recommendation			

	Cash Flows, Option 1		Cash Flows, Option 2	
	FIFO	LIFO	FIFO	LIFO
Sales				
Purchases				
Operating expenses				
Income taxes				
Cash flows				

Discussion:

Recommendations:

Chapter 10, SD 6. (Continued)

Chapter 10, SD 7.

1. Income statements and balance sheets prepared

RTS Company
Income Statement
For the Month Ended July 31, 20x4

	(a) FIFO	(b) LIFO

RTS Company
Balance Sheet
July 31, 20x4
(All figures in thousands)

Assets	(a) FIFO	(b) LIFO	Stockholders' Equity	(a) FIFO	(b) LIFO
Cash*			Common stock		
Inventory			Retained earnings		
Total assets			Total stockholders' equity		

Effects of each method:

				(a) FIFO	(b) LIFO
*Cash balance, July 1				$ 800	$ 800
Cash balance, July 31					

Chapter 10, SD 7. (Continued)

2. Dividend policy discussed

RTS Company
Balance Sheet
July 31, 20x4
(All figures in thousands)

Assets	FIFO	LIFO	Stockholders' Equity	FIFO	LIFO
Cash			Common stock		
Inventory			Total stockholders'		
Total assets			equity		

Discussion:

3. Consequences of additional price increase discussed

Chapter 10, SD 7. (Continued)

Chapter 10, FRA 1.

1. Schedule of net income (in millions)—**2000**

Net income (LIFO)		$334.0

Prices of cocoa and sugar:

2. LIFO discussed

Chapter 10, FRA 1. (Continued)

3. **Ratios computed** (in millions)

	LIFO	FIFO
Cost of goods sold		*
Average inventory		
Inventory turnover		
Average days' inventory on hand		

*See part 1.

Conclusion:

Chapter 10, FRA 2.

1.

2.

Chapter 10, FRA 3.

1.

2.

Chapter 10, FRA 4.

	Inventory Turnover*	=	
	Pioneer	=	
		=	
	Yamaha	=	
		=	

*Amounts are in millions.

	Average Days' Inventory on Hand	=	
	Pioneer	=	
	Yamaha	=	

Comments:

Chapter 10, FRA 5.

Inventory Turnover*	=	
2002	=	
	=	
2001	=	
	=	
Average Days' Inventory on Hand	=	
2002	=	
2001	=	

*Amounts are in millions.

Chapter 10, FRA 6.

1. **Inventory ratios calculated and discussed** (in thousands)

Toys "R" Us Inventory Turnover ratio:

Inventory Turnover	=	
2002	=	
	=	
2001	=	
	=	

Toys "R" Us Average Days' Inventory on Hand

Average Days' Inventory on Hand	=	
2002	=	
2001	=	

*Amounts are in millions.

Note to student: Ratios may be obtained from FRA 5.

Chapter 10, FRA 6. (Continued)

Walgreens Inventory Turnover ratio:

Inventory Turnover*	=	
2002	=	
	=	
2001	=	
	=	

Walgreens Average Days' Inventory on Hand

Average Days' Inventory on Hand	=	
2002	=	
2001	=	

*Amounts are in millions.

2. Inventory ratios discussed

Chapter 11, SE 1.

1.		4.	
2.		5.	
3.			

Chapter 11, SE 2.

1.		5.	
2.		6.	
3.		7.	
4.		8.	

Chapter 11, SE 3.

Asset	Appraisal	Percentage	Apportionment
Land	$200,000		
Land improvements	100,000		
Building	500,000		
Total	$800,000		

Chapter 11, SE 4.

Depreciation for each year:

Chapter 11, SE 5.

Depreciation for

Year 1:

Year 2:

Year 3:

Year 4:

Chapter 11, SE 6.

Depreciation for
- Year 1:
- Year 2:
- Year 3:
- Year 4:

Chapter 11, SE 7.

1. Carrying Value =
   =
   =

2. a. **Asset discarded, no cash received.**
      Gain (Loss) on Sale of Equipment =
      =
      =

   b. **Asset sold for $1,500 cash.**
      Gain (Loss) on Sale of Equipment =
      =
      =

   c. **Asset sold for $4,000 cash.**
      Gain (Loss) on Sale of Equipment =
      =
      =

Chapter 11, SE 8.

Carrying Value (Old) =
=
=

1. Exchange of dissimilar equipment with $3,800 trade-in allowance. New equipment recorded at $12,000 list price.

   Gain (Loss) on Exchange =
   =
   =

   Cash Payment =
   =
   =

2. Exchange of dissimilar equipment with $1,750 trade-in allowance. New equipment recorded at $12,000 list price.

   Gain (Loss) on Exchange =
   =
   =

   Cash Payment =
   =
   =

3. Exchange of similar equipment, no gain (loss) is recognized and cash paid as in 2 above.

   Equipment (New) =
   =
   =

Chapter 11, SE 9.

Depletion charge per ton:

Depletion expense for the first year:

Depreciation expense for the first year:

Chapter 11, SE 10.

Chapter 11, E 1.

1.		4.	
2.		5.	
3.		6.	

Chapter 11, E 2.

Calculation:	Present Value

Chapter 11, E 3.

Cost of land:

Cost of land improvements:

	should be debited to the Land account.
	should be debited to the Land Improvements account.

Chapter 11, E 4.

Asset	Value	Percentage	Apportionment*
Land			
Building			
Equipment			

Calculations:

Chapter 11, E 5.

Cost and depreciable cost of tractor:	

First year's depreciation:	

Chapter 11, E 6.

Cost	
Less estimated residual value	
Depreciable cost	

1.	Depreciation computed by straight-line method:

2.	Depreciation computed by production method:

3.	Depreciation computed by double-declining-balance method:
	20x4
	20x5

Adjusting entry:

Balance sheet presentation:

Chapter 11, E 7.

Year 1	
Year 2	
Year 3	
Year 4	

Chapter 11, E 8.

	Carrying Value	=	
		=	
		=	

1. **Asset discarded; no cash received.**

Gain (Loss) on Sale of Equipment	=	
	=	
	=	

2. **Asset sold for $6,000 cash.**

Gain (Loss) on Sale of Equipment	=	
	=	
	=	

3. **Asset sold for $18,000 cash.**

Gain (Loss) on Sale of Equipment	=	
	=	
	=	

4. **Exchange of dissimilar equipment with $16,200 trade-in allowance. New equipment recorded at $48,000 list price.**

Gain (Loss) on Sale of Equipment	=	
	=	
	=	

Cash Payment	=	
	=	
	=	

5. **Exchange of dissimilar equipment with $7,500 trade-in allowance. New equipment recorded at $48,000 list price.**

Gain (Loss) on Exchange	=	
	=	
	=	

Cash Payment	=	
	=	
	=	

6. **Exchange of similar equipment with $7,500 trade-in allowance. No gain (loss) is recognized; cash payment same as 5 above.**

Equipment (New)	=	
	=	
	=	

Chapter 11, E 9.

	20x7 July	1			
1.	20x7				
2.	20x7				
3.	20x7				
4.	20x7				

Chapter 11, E 9. (Continued)

5.	20x7			

6.	20x7			

7.	20x7			

8.	20x7			

9.	20x7			

Chapter 11, E 10.

1. Depletion charge per ton computed

Cost of land and ore	

2. Depletion expense computed

3. Depreciation expense determined for buildings

4. Depreciation expense determined for equipment

Chapter 11, E 11.

1.	Cost of copyright	
2.	Cost of trademark	

Chapter 11, E 12.

Cost	$90,000
Less estimated residual value	
Depreciable cost	

1.	Depreciation computed by straight-line method:
2.	Depreciation computed by production method:
3.	Depreciation computed by double-declining-balance method:
	20x4:

Chapter 11, E 13.	
Cost	
Residual value	
Depreciable cost	

First-year depreciation:

Second-year depreciation:

Depreciation to date	

Remaining depreciable cost:

Remaining useful life:

Third-year depreciation:

Chapter 11, E 14.
1.
2.
3.
4.
5.
6.

Chapter 11, E 15.

1. Entry prepared to record cost of repair

2. Carrying value computed

3. Depreciation entry prepared

Chapter 11, P 1.

Constanza Computers
Schedule of Proper Charges for Training Center
December 31, 20x4

	Land	Land Improvements	Building	Furniture and Equipment
Attorney's fee	$ 17,450			
Totals				

Chapter 11, P 2.

1. Depreciation computed

Depreciation Table

	Depreciation Method	Year	Computation				Depreciation	Carrying Value
a.	Straight-line	1	$660,000	x	1	/ 4		
		2						
		3						
		4						
b.	Production	1		x				
		2		x				
		3		x				
		4		x				
c.	Double-declining-balance	1	$720,000	x	1	/ 2		
		2						
		3						
		4						

2. Adjusting entry prepared—straight-line method

Chapter 11, P 2. (Continued)

3. Balance sheet presentation after two years shown

4. Conclusions drawn from depreciation patterns

Chapter 11, P 3.

Asset	Year	Computations								Depreciation 20x5	20x6	20x7
Washing machines	20x5	$14,400	x	1	/	4	x	10	/ 12	$ 3,000		
	20x6											
	20x7											
Tanning machine	20x5	$36,000	x	2,100 / 7,500								
	20x6		x									
	20x7		x									
Refreshment center	20x5	$4,000	x	0.2	x	3	/	12				
	20x6											
	20x7											
Total Depreciation Expense												

Chapter 11, P 4.

a.

Chapter 11, P 4. (Continued)

Chapter 11, P 5.

Part A. Entries prepared in journal form

a.

Chapter 11, P 5. (Continued)

Part B. Entries prepared in journal form

a.

Chapter 11, P 6.

Patroni Company
Schedule of Proper Charges to Asset and Expense Accounts
December 31, 20x5

	Land	Land Improvements	Buildings	Machinery	Expense
Land	$633,200				
Totals					

Chapter 11, P 7.

1. Depreciation computed

Depreciation Table

	Depreciation Method	Year	Computation				Depreciation	Carrying Value
a.	Straight-line	1	$325,500	x	1	/ 6		
		2						
		3						
		4						
		5						
		6						
b.	Production	1		x				
		2		x				
		3		x				
		4		x				
		5		x				
		6		x				
c.	Double-declining-balance	1	$360,500	x	1	/ 3	*	
		2						
		3					*	
		4						
		5					*	
		6						

*Rounded.

Chapter 11, P 7. (Continued)

2. Adjusting entry prepared—straight-line method

3. Balance sheet presentation after two years shown

4. Conclusions drawn from depreciation patterns

Chapter 11, P 8.

Equipment No.	Computations			Depreciation 20x4	20x5	20x6
1	$180,000	x	0.2			
2						
3						
Total Depreciation Expense						

Chapter 11, SD 1.

Chapter 11, SD 2.

(continued)

Chapter 11, SD 2. (Continued)

Chapter 11, SD 3.

Chapter 11, SD 4.

Chapter 11, SD 5.

Chapter 11, SD 5. (Continued)

Chapter 11, SD 7.

1. Present value computed for each type of equipment

Type A

Type B

2. Net present value computed for each type of equipment

Type A

Net Present Value =

Type B

	Net Cash Receipts	x	Factor*	=	Present Value
Year 1		x		=	
Year 2		x		=	
Year 3		x		=	
Year 4		x		=	
Year 5		x		=	
Total Present Value					
Net Present Value =					

Chapter 11, SD 7. (Continued)

3. Memorandum with recommendation

Memorandum	
Date:	Today's Date
To:	Board of Directors
From:	Student
Re:	Purchase Recommendation

Chapter 11, FRA 1.

1. Changes explained

2. Conservatism and earnings quality discussed

Chapter 11, FRA 1. (Continued)

Chapter 11, FRA 2.

Chapter 11, FRA 3.

1.

2.

3.

Chapter 11, FRA 4.

1. Growth of property and equipment analyzed

(In millions, except percentages)

	Total Property and Equipment		Net Additions (Capital Expenditures)		Percentage	
	2002	2001	2002	2001	2002	2001
Toys "R" Us						
Walgreens						

2. Other cash flow requirements discussed

Chapter 12, SE 1.

1.		3.		5.	
2.		4.			

Chapter 12, SE 2.

Working Capital	=	
	=	
Payables Turnover	=	
	=	
	=	
Average Days' Payable	=	=

Chapter 12, SE 3.

1.		4.		7.	
2.		5.			
3.		6.			

Chapter 12, SE 4.

1.	Aug.	31			
2.					

Chapter 12, SE 5.

1.	Aug.	31			

Chapter 12, SE 6.

1.	Apr.	30			

Chapter 12, SE 7.

Oct.	31			

Chapter 12, SE 8.

Vacation pay expense for September:

Chapter 12, SE 9.

	Taxes Paid by Employees	Taxes Paid by Employer

Chapter 12, SE 10.

Chapter 12, E 1.

1.	4.	7.
2.	5.	8.
3.	6.	

Chapter 12, E 2.

20x1:

Working Capital =

=

Payables Turnover =

=

=

Average Days' Payable =   =

20x2:

Working Capital =

=

Payables Turnover =

=

=

Average Days' Payable =   =

Assessment:

Chapter 12, E 3.

1.	Oct.	31			

Chapter 12, E 4.

1.	Oct.	31			

Chapter 12, E 5.

1. Amount of revenue determined

Revenue for the month:

2. Entry in journal form prepared

Aug.	31			

Chapter 12, E 6.

1.	Oct.	31			

Chapter 12, E 7.

1. Estimated liability recorded

July	31			

2. Games' replacement recorded

July	31			

Chapter 12, E 8.

1. Employee benefit for July vacation estimated

2 and 3. Entries in journal form prepared

July	31			

Chapter 12, E 9.

1. Schedule of employee earnings prepared

Munro Company
Schedule of Wages Subject to Payroll Taxes

Employee Name	Cumulative Earnings	Earnings Subject to Social Security Tax	Earnings Subject to Medicare Tax	Earnings Subject to Unemployment Taxes
Basmani, J.	$ 28,620			
Cohen, A.	5,260			
Derbye, G.	32,820			
Carbone, R.	30,130			
Sourdiffe, B.	89,000			
Conniger, N.	5,120			
Van Trapp, M.	16,760			
Harwit, P.	6,420			
Lemaire, C.	51,650			
Papyani, D.	32,100			
Menzek, V.	36,645			
Woo, S.	5,176			
Totals				

2. Social security, Medicare, and unemployment taxes computed

Social security tax	
Employees' share:	
Employer's share:	
Total social security tax	
Medicare tax	
Employees' share:	
Employer's share:	
Total Medicare tax	
State unemployment tax	
Federal unemployment tax	

Chapter 12, E 10.

1. Employee's net pay computed

a. Total pay

    Total pay

b. Federal income taxes withheld:

c. Social security tax:

   Medicare tax:

d. Net pay

    Total pay

       Less:

    Net pay

2. Entry prepared in journal form

20xx				
July	11			

Chapter 12, E 11.

1. Entry summarizing employee's pay prepared in journal form

Salaries Expense		

2. Entry for payroll expenses prepared in journal form

3. Cost of employee determined

Chapter 12, P 1.

1. Current liabilities determined

2. Additional information identified

Chapter 12, P 1. (Continued)

3. Liquidity ratios computed and evaluated (cents omitted)

Working Capital	=	
	=	
Payables Turnover	=	
	=	
	=	
Average Days' Payable	=	=

Commont on the results:

Chapter 12, P 2.

1. Transactions recorded

20x3				

2. Loan options discussed

Chapter 12, P 3.

1. Entries prepared in journal form

a. Sept. 30

2. Balance of Estimated Product Warranty Liability account computed

3. Product warranty liability estimation discussed

Chapter 12, P 4.

1.–4. Entries prepared in journal form

	20xx				
1.	Oct.	31			

Chapter 12, P 5.

1. Payroll register prepared

Payroll Register

Pay Period: November 30

Employee	Earnings				Deductions			Supplemental Benefits Plan	Net Pay	Distribution		Administrative Salaries Expense
	Total Hours	Regular	Overtime	Gross	Cumulative	Federal Income Taxes	Social Security Tax	Medicare Tax			Sales Wages Expense	
Eggers, D.												
Gosligan, W.												
Valmont, P.												
Norelli, V.												
Appia, L.												
Tou, M.												
Voss, B.												

Chapter 12, P 5. (Continued)

2, 3, and 4. Entries prepared in journal form

20xx Nov.	30			

Chapter 12, P 6.

1. Transactions recorded

20xx				
May	11			

2. Loan options discussed

Chapter 12, P 7.

1. Entries prepared in journal form

a. June 30

2. Balance of Estimated Product Warranty Liability account computed

3. Product warranty liability estimation discussed

Chapter 12, P 8.

1.–4. Entries prepared in journal form

1.	Apr.	30			

Chapter 12, SD 2.

Chapter 12, SD 5.

1. The current liabilities of Miller Bicycles as of December 31, 20x4, are as follows:

2.

Chapter 12, FRA 1.

Payables Turnover*	=	
Sun Microsystems	=	
	=	
Cisco Systems	=	
	=	
Average Days' Payable	=	
Sun Microsystems	=	
Cisco Systems	=	

*Amounts are in thousands.

Chapter 12, FRA 2.

1. FASB conditions discussed

2. Events of 1987 discussed

3. Effect of settlement discussed

Chapter 12, FRA 3.

Chapter 12, FRA 4.

Payables Turnover =

=

=

=

Discussion:

Chapter 12, FRA 5.

1. Payables ratios calculated and compared (in millions)

Toys "R" Us's Payables Turnover ratio:

Payables Turnover	=	
2002	=	
	=	
2001	=	
	=	

Toys "R" Us's Average Days' Payable:

Average Days' Payable	=	
2002	=	
2001	=	

Walgreens' Payables Turnover ratio:

Payables Turnover	=	
2002	=	
	=	
2001	=	
	=	

Walgreens' Average Days' Payable:

Average Days' Payable	=	
2002	=	
2001	=	

Chapter 12, FRA 5. (Continued)

2. Commitments and contingencies discussed

Chapter 13, SE 1.

1.
2.
3.
4.
5.

Chapter 13, SE 2.

Chapter 13, SE 3.

Computation of capital ratios:

Division of income:

Chapter 13, SE 4.

	Income of Partner		Income Distributed
	Bob	Kim	
Total Income for Distribution			$5,000
Income of Partners			

Chapter 13, SE 5.

	Income (Loss) of Partner		Income Distributed
	Bob	Kim	
Total Income for Distribution			

Chapter 13, SE 6.

Capital account balances:

Chapter 13, SE 7.

New Capital account balances:
Bob
Kim
Sonia

Chapter 13, SE 8.

New Capital account balances:
Bob
Kim
Sonia

Chapter 13, SE 9.

Chapter 13, SE 10.

Loss on office equipment computed:

	Bob	Kim
Distribution of Cash to Partners		

Chapter 13, E 1.

Chapter 13, E 2.

1. Computation: The partners share equally.
    Samuels
    Winslow
Total net income

2. Computation: The partners agreed to share the income three-fifths to Samuels and two-fifths to Winslow.
    Samuels
    Winslow
Total net income

3. Computation: The partners agreed to share the income in the ratio of their original investments.
    Samuels
    Winslow
Total net income

4. Computation:

	Income of Partner		Income Distributed
	Samuels	Winslow	

Chapter 13, E 3.

1. Computation:

	Income (Loss) of Partner		Income Distributed
	Samuels	Winslow	

2. Computation:

	Income (Loss) of Partner		Income Distributed
	Samuels	Winslow	

Chapter 13, E 3. (Continued)

3.	Computation:	Income (Loss) of Partner		Loss Distributed
		Samuels	Winslow	

4.	Computation:	Income (Loss) of Partner		Loss Distributed
		Samuels	Winslow	

Chapter 13, E 4.

Average capital balances computed

Partner	Date	Capital Balance	x	Months Unchanged	=	Total		Average Capital
Barbara	Jan.–Mar.		x		=			
	Apr.–Dec.		x		=			
Karen	Jan.–Sept.		x		=			
	Oct.–Dec.		x		=			
					Total average capital			

Average capital balance ratios computed

Barbara	=	
Karen	=	

Distribution of income computed

Barbara	=	
Karen	=	

Chapter 13, E 5.

1.

Computation:

Bonus to the original partners

Distribution of bonus to original partners:	
Ernie	
Ron	
Denis	
Total bonus	

Chapter 13, E 5. (Continued)

2.

Computation:

Distribution of bonus from original partners:		
Ernie		
Ron		
Denis		
Total bonus		

Chapter 13, E 6.

Computation:

Distribution of bonus from remaining partners:

Danny	
Steve	
Total bonus	

Chapter 13, E 7.

1. Cash distribution to partners calculated

Ming and Demmick
Statement of Liquidation
December 31, 20xx

Explanation	Cash	Other Assets	Liabilities	Ming, Capital (75%)	Demmick, Capital (25%)	Gain (or Loss) from Realization
Balance, December 31, 20xx	—	$160,000	$10,000	$90,000	$60,000	
Sale of Assets						
Payment of Liabilities						
Distribution of Gain (or Loss) from Realization						
Distribution of Cash to Partners						

Calculation:

Ming	x	/
Demmick	x	/

Chapter 13, E 7. (Continued)

2. Entries prepared in journal form

Chapter 13, E 8.

Ariel, Mandy, and Tisha
Statement of Liquidation
July 1, 20x7

Explanation	Cash	Other Assets	Liabilities	Ariel, Capital (__%)	Mandy, Capital (__%)	Tisha, Capital (__%)	Gain (or Loss) from Realization
Balance, July 1, 20x7	—	$480,000	$160,000	$140,000	$40,000	$140,000	—
Sale of Assets							
Payment of Liabilities							
Distribution of Gain (or Loss) from Realization							
Distribution of Partners' Share of Mandy's Deficit							
Distribution of Cash to Partners							

Chapter 13, P 1.

1. Entry prepared

2. Share of income for each partner determined

a. Income shared equally

	20x3	20x4
Rivera		
Bacon		
Totals		

b. No agreement

c. Income shared on the basis of the partners' original investments

	20x3	20x4
Rivera		
Bacon		
Totals		

Chapter 13, P 1. (Continued)

d. Interest on investments; remainder shared equally

20x3 computation:	Income of Partner		Income Distributed
	Rivera	Bacon	
Total Income for Distribution			
Remaining Income			
Income of Partners			

20x4 computation:	Income of Partner		Income Distributed
	Rivera	Bacon	
Total Income for Distribution			
Remaining Income			
Income of Partners			

Chapter 13, P 1. (Continued)

e. **Salaries allowed; remainder shared equally**

20x3 computation:	Income of Partner		Income Distributed
	Rivera	Bacon	
Total Income for Distribution			
Remaining Income			
Income of Partners			

20x4 computation:	Income of Partner		Income Distributed
	Rivera	Bacon	
Total Income for Distribution			
Remaining Income			
Income of Partners			

Chapter 13, P 1. (Continued)

	f.	Interest and salaries allowed; remainder shared equally			
		20x3 computation:	**Income of Partner**		**Income Distributed**
			Rivera	Bacon	
		Total Income for Distribution			
		Remaining Income			
		Income of Partners			
		20x4 computation:	**Income of Partner**		**Income Distributed**
			Rivera	Bacon	
		Total Income for Distribution			
		Remaining Income			
		Income of Partners			

Chapter 13, P 1. (Continued)

3. Income sharing factors discussed

Chapter 13, P 2.

1. Income distribution calculated for income of $168,000

	Income of Partner		Income Distributed
	Naomi	Petri	
Total Income for Distribution			$168,000
Remaining Income			
Income of Partners			

2. Income distribution calculated for income of $88,000

	Income of Partner		Income Distributed
	Naomi	Petri	
Total Income for Distribution			$88,000
Remaining Income			
Income of Partners			

Chapter 13, P 2. (Continued)

3. Distribution calculated for $25,600 loss

	Income (Loss) of Partner		Loss Distributed
	Naomi	Petri	
Total Loss for Distribution			
Remaining Loss			
Income and Loss of Partners			

Chapter 13, P 3.

1. Partnership transactions recorded

a.

Computation:

Bonus to the original partners

Distribution of bonus to original partners:

Marnie	
Stacie	
Samantha	
Total bonus	

Chapter 13, P 3. (Continued)

	Partners' capital ratios:		
	Partner	Capital Balance	Ratios
	Marnie		
	Stacie		
	Samantha		

d.	July	31				

Computation:

Distribution of bonus from original partners:

Marnie		
Stacie		
Samantha		
Total bonus		

Chapter 13, P 3. (Continued)

e.	July	31			

Distribution of excess cash over Marnie's capital balance between the remaining partners:

Stacie			
Samantha			
Total			

f.	July	31			

2. Motivation for bonuses discussed

Chapter 13, P 4.

1. Statement of liquidation prepared

Caruso, Evans, and Weisman Partnership
Statement of Liquidation
September 1–11, 20x7

Explanation	Cash	Other Assets	Accounts Payable	Caruso, Capital (__%)	Evans, Capital (__%)	Weisman, Capital (__%)	Gain (or Loss) from Realization
Balance, August 31, 20x7	$ 280,000	$880,000	$360,000	$400,000	$240,000	$160,000	
a.							
b.							
c.							
d.							

Chapter 13, P 4. (Continued)

2. Entries prepared

a. Sept. 1

Chapter 13, P 5.					
20x4					
Feb.	14				

Computation:	Income of Partner		Income Distributed
	Raymond	Bryden	
Total Income for Distribution			$ 84,000
Remaining Income			
Income of Partners			

Chapter 13, P 5. (Continued)

20x5 Jan.	1			

Computation:

Bonus to Menzer	

Distribution of bonus from original partners:	
Raymond	
Bryden	
Total bonus	

Chapter 13, P 5. (Continued)

20x5					
Dec.	31				

Computation:	Income (Loss) of Partner			Income Distributed
	Raymond	Bryden	Menzer	
Total Income for Distribution				$ 87,200
Remaining Income				
Income and Loss of Partners				

Chapter 13, P 5. (Continued)

20x6				
Jan.	1			

Chapter 13, P 5. (Continued)

Raymond, Bryden, and Menzer Partnership
Statement of Liquidation
January 1, 20x6

Explanation	Cash	Accounts Receivable (net)	Land	Building (net)	Equipment (net)	Accounts Payable	Mortgage Payable	Raymond, Capital (33.3%)	Bryden, Capital (33.3%)	Menzer, Capital (33.3%)	Gain (or Loss) from Realization
Balance 1/1/x6											

Chapter 13, P 6.

1. Income distribution calculated for income of $545,200

	Income of Partner			Income Distributed
	Jacob	Deric	Jason	
Total Income for Distribution				$545,200
Remaining Income				
Income of Partners				

2. Income distribution calculated for income of $155,600

	Income of Partner			Income Distributed
	Jacob	Deric	Jason	
Total Income for Distribution				$155,600
Remaining Income				
Income of Partners				

Chapter 13, P 6. (Continued)

3. Distribution calculated for $56,800 loss

	Income (Loss) of Partner			Loss Distributed
	Jacob	Deric	Jason	
Total Loss for Distribution				($ 56,800)
Remaining Loss				
Income and Loss of Partners				

Chapter 13, P 7.

1. Partnership transactions recorded

a. Nov. 30

Computation:

Bonus to the original partners

Distribution of bonus to original partners:
Peter
Mara
Vanessa
Total bonus

Chapter 13, P 7. (Continued)

d.	Nov.	30			
	Computation:				
	Distribution of bonus from original partners to Bob:				
	Total bonus				
e.	Nov.	30			
	Distribution between the remaining partners of excess cash over Peter's capital balance:				
	Total				
f.	Nov.	30			

Chapter 13, P 7. (Continued)

2. Motivation for bonuses discussed

Chapter 13, P 8.

1. Statement of liquidation prepared

Rose Partnership
Statement of Liquidation
July 31, 20xx

Explanation	Cash	Accounts Receivable	Inventory	Equipment (net)	Accounts Payable	Gerri, Capital (__%)	Susi, Capital (__%)	Mari, Capital (__%)	Gain (or Loss) from Realization
Balance, 7/31/xx									
a.									

Chapter 13, P 8. (Continued)

2. Entries prepared

a.	July	31			

Chapter 13, SD 2.

Memorandum

Date:
To:
From:
Re:

Chapter 13, SD 5.

1.

2.

	20x3	20x4	20x5	20x6	20x7
Projected income before salaries					

3.

4.

Chapter 13, FRA 1.

1.

2.

Chapter 13, FRA 2.

Chapter 14, SE 1.

1.
2.
3.
4.
5.
6.

Chapter 14, SE 2.

1.
2.
3.
4.
5.
6.

Chapter 14, SE 3.

Start-up and Organization Costs	
Income Statement Effect	
Balance Sheet Effect	

Chapter 14, SE 4.

June	6			

Chapter 14, SE 5.

Keech Corporation
Balance Sheet
December 31, 20xx
Stockholders' Equity

Chapter 14, SE 6.

May	15			

Chapter 14, SE 7.

	Preferred Stock Dividends		Common Stock Dividends		Total Dividends Allocated
	Amount	Per Share	Amount	Per Share	
20x3	——	——	——	——	——
20x4					
Totals					
20x5					
Totals					

Chapter 14, SE 8.

1.

2.

Chapter 14, SE 9.

1.

2.

Chapter 14, SE 10.

Oct.	1			

Chapter 14, SE 11.

Oct.	28			

Chapter 14, E 1.

Dividends Yield = ──────────

= ──────────

Price/Earnings (P/E) Ratio = ──────────

= ──────────

Chapter 14, E 2.

Halloran Corporation
Balance Sheet
December 31, 20xx
Stockholders' Equity

Chapter 14, E 3.

1.		4.		7.	
2.		5.		8.	
3.		6.		9.	

Chapter 14, E 4.

1. Transactions recorded in T accounts

Preferred Stock		Common Stock	
Cash		Paid-in Capital in Excess of Stated Value, Common	

2. Stockholders' equity section of the balance sheet prepared

Wallace Hospital Supply Corporation
Balance Sheet
March 1, 20xx
Stockholders' Equity

Chapter 14, E 5.

June	5			

Chapter 14, E 6.

Oct.	15			

Chapter 14, E 7.

	Preferred Stock Dividends		Common Stock Dividends		Total Dividends Allocated
	Amount	Per Share	Amount	Per Share	
20x3	—	—	—	—	—
20x4					
Totals					
20x5					
Totals					
20x6					
Totals					

Chapter 14, E 8.

	Preferred Stock Dividends	Common Stock Dividends	Total
1. 20x3 dividends			
2. 20x3 dividends			
Totals			

Chapter 14, E 9.

1. Entry prepared—$25 par value

Aug.	1			

2. Entry prepared—$10 par value

Aug.	1			

3. Entry prepared—no par value

Aug.	1			

4. Entry prepared—$1 stated value

Aug.	1			

Chapter 14, E 10.

1. Entry prepared—$10 par value

20xx				
July	1			

2. Entry prepared—no par value

20xx				
July	1			

3. Entry prepared—$4 stated value

20xx				
July	1			

Chapter 14, E 11.

Cash		Treasury Stock, Common	
		Paid-in Capital, Treasury Stock	

Chapter 14, E 12.

Cash		Treasury Stock, Common	

Retained Earnings		Paid-in Capital, Treasury Stock	

Common Stock		Paid-in Capital in Excess of Par Value, Common	

Chapter 14, P 1.

1. Transactions recorded in T accounts

Cash	Common Stock

Cash Dividends Declared	Cash Dividends Payable

Paid-in Capital in Excess of Par Value, Common	Start-up and Organization Expense

Retained Earnings	

Chapter 14, P 1. (Continued)

2. Stockholders' equity section of balance sheet prepared

<table>
<tr><td colspan="2" align="center">Jung Corporation
Balance Sheet
May 31, 20xx</td></tr>
<tr><td colspan="2" align="center">Stockholders' Equity</td></tr>
<tr><td></td><td></td></tr>
</table>

Chapter 14, P 2.

1. Dividends calculated for cumulative preferred stock and common stock

	Cumulative Preferred Stock Dividends		Common Stock Dividends		Total Dividends Allocated
	Amount	Per Share	Amount	Per Share	
20x3					

2. Dividends calculated for noncumulative preferred stock and common stock

	Noncumulative Preferred Stock Dividends		Common Stock Dividends		Total Dividends Allocated
	Amount	Per Share	Amount	Per Share	
20x3					
20x4					
20x5					
20x6					

3. The 20x5 and 20x6 dividends yield for common stock calculated

	20x5	20x6	

Chapter 14, P 2. (Continued)

4. Preferred stock compared to long-term bonds

Chapter 14, P 3.

1. Treasury stock transactions recorded

Chapter 14, P 3. (Continued)

2. Effects of treasury stock purchase discussed

Chapter 14, P 4.

1. Transactions recorded in T accounts

Preferred Stock		Common Stock	

Paid-in Capital in Excess of Stated Value, Common		Treasury Stock, Common	

Cash Dividends Payable		Cash Dividends Declared	

Start-up and Organization Expense		Land	

Cash	

Chapter 14, P 4. (Continued)

2. Stockholders' equity section of the balance sheet prepared

Arkazian, Inc.
Balance Sheet
August 31, 20xx
Stockholders' Equity

3. Ratios computed

Dividends Yield =

Price/Earnings Ratio =

Return on Equity =

Chapter 14, P 5.

1. Transactions recorded in T accounts

Cash	Land
	Building
Cash Dividends Payable	**Preferred Stock**
Common Stock	**Paid-in Capital in Excess of Stated Value, Common**
Paid-in Capital, Treasury Stock	**Retained Earnings**
Treasury Stock, Common	**Cash Dividends Declared**
Start-up and Organization Expense	

Chapter 14, P 5. (Continued)

2. Stockholders' equity section of the balance sheet prepared

<table>
<tr><td colspan="3" align="center">Hammond Corporation
Balance Sheet
December 31, 20xx</td></tr>
<tr><td colspan="3" align="center">Stockholders' Equity</td></tr>
<tr><td></td><td></td><td></td></tr>
</table>

Chapter 14, P 6.

1. Entries prepared in journal form

Sept.	1			

Chapter 14, P 6. (Continued)

2. Stockholders' equity section of the balance sheet prepared

Quesnel Corporation
Balance Sheet
November 30, 20xx

Stockholders' Equity

Chapter 14, P 7.

1. **Dividends calculated for cumulative preferred stock and common stock**

	Cumulative Preferred Stock Dividends		Common Stock Dividends		Total Dividends Allocated
	Amount	Per Share	Amount	Per Share	
20x2					

2. **Dividends calculated for noncumulative preferred stock and common stock**

	Noncumulative Preferred Stock Dividends		Common Stock Dividends		Total Dividends Allocated
	Amount	Per Share	Amount	Per Share	
20x2					
20x3					
20x4					

3. **The 20x3 and 20x4 dividends yield for common stock calculated**

	20x3	20x4	

Chapter 14, P 7. (Continued)

4. Preferred stock compared to long-term bonds

Chapter 14, P 8.

1. Transactions recorded in journal form

July	1			

Chapter 14, P 8. (Continued)

2. Stockholders' equity section of the balance sheet prepared

Czerepak, Inc. **Balance Sheet** **August 31, 20xx**		
Stockholders' Equity		

Chapter 14, SD 1.

Chapter 14, SD 2.

Chapter 14, SD 3.

Effects of buybacks:

Ratio	Effect	Favorable or Unfavorable
Earnings per share		
Return on equity		
Return on assets		
Debt to equity		
Current ratio		

Chapter 14, SD 6.

1. Schedule of alternatives prepared

<table>
<tr><th colspan="4">Northeast Servotech Corporation
Schedule of Financing Alternatives
20xx</th></tr>
<tr><th></th><th colspan="3">Alternatives</th></tr>
<tr><th></th><th>A</th><th>B</th><th>C</th></tr>
<tr><td></td><td></td><td></td><td></td></tr>
<tr><td></td><td></td><td></td><td></td></tr>
<tr><td></td><td></td><td></td><td></td></tr>
<tr><td></td><td></td><td></td><td></td></tr>
<tr><td></td><td></td><td></td><td></td></tr>
<tr><td></td><td></td><td></td><td></td></tr>
<tr><td></td><td></td><td></td><td></td></tr>
<tr><td></td><td></td><td></td><td></td></tr>
<tr><td></td><td></td><td></td><td></td></tr>
<tr><td></td><td></td><td></td><td></td></tr>
<tr><td></td><td></td><td></td><td></td></tr>
<tr><td>Debt to equity ratio</td><td></td><td></td><td></td></tr>
</table>

Chapter 14, SD 6. (Continued)

2. Cash requirements for the first year computed

Alternative A

Alternative B

Alternative C

3. Cash requirements in future years discussed

Chapter 14, SD 6. (Continued)

4. **Memorandum prepared**

Memorandum
Date:
To:
From:
Re:

Chapter 14, FRA 1.

1. Stock issue recorded in journal form

2. Stockholders' equity section of the balance sheet prepared

Netscape Communications Corporation
Balance Sheet
After Stock Offering
Stockholders' Equity
(in thousands)

Chapter 14, FRA 1. (Continued)

3. Netscape's need to increase the authorized shares discussed

4. Underwriters' fee discussed

Chapter 14, FRA 2.

Chapter 14, FRA 3.

(Answers are in millions of Swiss francs, except per share amounts)

Dividends per Share =

 =

Dividends Yield =

 =

Increase in retained earnings plus dividends = 2001 earnings

In U.S. dollars:

Return on Equity =

 =

 =

Comments:

Chapter 14, FRA 4.

1.

2.

3.

4.

(continued)

Chapter 14, FRA 4. (Continued)

Price/Earnings Ratio	=	
2002	=	
2001	=	

The return on equity increased as follows:

Return on Equity	=	
2002	=	
	=	
	=	
2001	=	
	=	
	=	

Chapter 14, FRA 5.

1. Return on equity computed (dollars in millions)

Toys "R" Us's Return on Equity ratio:

Return on Equity	=	
2002	=	
	=	
	=	
2001	=	
	=	
	=	

Walgreens' Return on Equity ratio:

Return on Equity	=	
2002	=	
	=	
	=	
2001	=	
	=	
	=	

Chapter 14, FRA 5. (Continued)

2. Treasury stock purchases discussed

3. Stock issues discussed

4. Dividend policies discussed

Chapter 15, SE 1.

1.
2.
3.
4.
5.
6.
7.
8.

Chapter 15, SE 2.

Bedard Company
Income Statement
For the Year Ended June 30, 20xx

Chapter 15, SE 3.

1.	Taxable income of	$400,000

2.	Taxable income of	$20,000,000

Chapter 15, SE 4.

Weighted-average number of common shares computed:

20x4	
20x5	

Earnings per share computed:

	20x4	20x5

Chapter 15, SE 5.

1.
2.
3.
4.

Chapter 15, SE 6.

	Total Assets	Total Liabilities	Total Stockholders' Equity	
1.				
2.				
3.				
4.				
5.				

Chapter 15, SE 7.

Chapter 15, SE 8.

Feb.	15			

Chapter 15, SE 9.

After Stock Split

Torrinni International **Stockholders' Equity** **August 10, 20xx**	

Chapter 15, SE 10.

Preferred Stock Book Value per Share	=	
	=	
Common Stock Book Value per Share	=	
	=	

Chapter 15, E 1.

1. **Net income determined under FIFO**

2. **Net income determined under LIFO**

3.

4.

5.

Chapter 15, E 2.

Sedgeway Furniture Company
Income Statement
For the Year Ended June 30, 20xx

Net sales		$1,900,000

Chapter 15, E 3.

Asheville Corporation
Income Statement
For the Year Ended December 31, 20x4

Sales		$555,000

Earnings per common share:

Chapter 15, E 4.

Situation A

Situation B

Situation C

Chapter 15, E 5.

1. Amount of income taxes paid computed

	20x2	20x3

2. Entries prepared in journal form

20x2		

Chapter 15, E 6.

1. Weighted-average number of common shares computed

20x3		
20x4		

2. Earnings per share computed

	20x3	20x4

Chapter 15, E 7.

Chapter 15, E 8.

Mallory Corporation
Statement of Stockholders' Equity
For the Year Ended December 31, 20x5

	9%, $100 Par Value Cumulative Preferred Stock	$2 Par Value Common Stock	Paid-in Capital in Excess of Par Value, Common	Retained Earnings	Treasury Stock	Other Accumulated Comprehensive Income	Total
Balance, December 31, 20x4							
a.							
Balance, December 31, 20x5							

Chapter 15, E 9.

July	17			

Chapter 15, E 10.

Before Stock Split

Teuong Company Stockholders' Equity May 15, 20xx	

After Stock Split

Teuong Company Stockholders' Equity May 15, 20xx	

Chapter 15, E 11.

Before Stock Split

Exavier International
Stockholders' Equity
January 15, 20xx

After Stock Split

Exavier International
Stockholders' Equity
January 15, 20xx

Chapter 15, E 12.

Preferred Stock Book Value per Share	=	
	=	
Common Stock Book Value per Share	=	
	=	

Chapter 15, P 1.

1. Alternative income statements prepared

Carsey Company
Alternative Income Statements
For the Year Ended December 31, 20xx

Income Statement Using FIFO and Straight-Line Methods

Net sales			$650,000

Income Statement Using LIFO and Double-Declining-Balance Methods

Net sales			$650,000

Chapter 15, P 1. (Continued)

2. Schedule prepared

Carsey Company
Schedule of Differences in Net Income
For the Year Ended December 31, 20xx

3. Inventory turnover computed and discussed

Inventory Turnover	FIFO Method	LIFO Method

Conclusions:

Chapter 15, P 1. (Continued)

4. Return on assets computed and discussed

		Return on Assets
		FIFO/SL Methods
	=	
	=	
		LIFO/DDB Methods
	=	
	=	

Chapter 15, P 2.

1. **Income statement prepared**

Dimsum Corporation
Income Statement
For the Year Ended December 31, 20x3

Net sales		

Earnings per common share:	

2. **Restructuring charge discussed**

Chapter 15, P 3.

1. Income statement prepared

Burston Corporation
Income Statements
For the Years Ended December 31, 20x3 and 20x2

	20x3	20x2
Net sales	$3,500,000	$4,200,000

Earnings per common share:

Chapter 15, P 3. (Continued)

2. Plan assessed

Chapter 15, P 4.

1. Transactions recorded in T accounts

Common Stock	Common Stock Distributable

Paid-in Capital in Excess of Par Value, Common	Retained Earnings

Stock Dividends Declared	

Chapter 15, P 4. (Continued)

2. Stockholders' equity section of the balance sheet prepared

Montpelior Linen Mills, Inc.
Stockholders' Equity
December 31, 20x3

3. Book value per share calculated

Dec. 31, 20x2:

Dec. 31, 20x3:

Chapter 15, P 5.

1. Transactions recorded in journal form

20x3				

Chapter 15, P 5. (Continued)

2. Stockholders' equity section of the balance sheet prepared

O'Malley Woolen Company
Stockholders' Equity
September 30, 20x4

Retained earnings (Note *x*)

Note *x*:

3. Book value per share calculated

Sept. 30, 20x3:

Sept. 30, 20x4:

Chapter 15, P 6.

1. Income statement prepared

	MacFarland Weather Gear Corporation Income Statement For the Year Ended December 31, 20xx		
Net sales			$975,000
Earnings per common share:			

2. Write-down discussed

Chapter 15, P 7.

1. Transactions recorded in T accounts

Common Stock		Paid-in Capital in Excess of Par Value, Common	

Common Stock Distributable		Stock Dividends Declared	

Treasury Stock		Retained Earnings	

Chapter 15, P 7. (Continued)

2. Stockholders' equity section of the balance sheet prepared

Boysan Corporation
Stockholders' Equity
December 31, 20x5

3. Book value per share calculated

Dec. 31, 20x4:

Dec. 31, 20x5:

Chapter 15, P 8.

1. Transactions recorded in journal form

20x3				
Mar.	5			

Chapter 15, P 8. (Continued)

2. Stockholders' equity section of the balance sheet prepared

Blue Ridge Furniture Restoration Company
Stockholders' Equity
December 31, 20x3

Note x:

3. Book value per share calculated

Dec. 31, 20x2:
Dec. 31, 20x3:

Chapter 15, SD 1.

Chapter 15, SD 3.

Chapter 15, SD 5.

1. Stockholders' equity section prepared (in thousands of dollars)

	Common Stock		
	Common Stock Distributable		
	Paid-in Capital in Excess of Par Value, Common		
	Retained Earnings		
	Treasury Stock, Common		
	Common Stock Outstanding (in thousands of shares)		

Chapter 15, SD 5. (Continued)

Metzger Steel Corporation Stockholders' Equity December 31, 20x5 (in thousands)	

Chapter 15, SD 5. (Continued)

2. Arnold Metzger's position analyzed and discussed

Memorandum

Date:
To:
From:
Re:

Arnold Metzger's shares:

Book value computations, December 31, 20x4

Book value computations, December 31, 20x5 (after stock dividend)

Chapter 15, SD 5. (Continued)

Chapter 15, FRA 1.

1. Entries prepared in journal form

Chapter 15, FRA 1. (Continued)

2. Entries discussed

Chapter 15, FRA 2.

1. **Income taxes expense computed** (in millions) **and entry in journal form to record income taxes prepared**

Current income tax provision	
Deferred income tax provision	
Income taxes expense on the income statement	

2. **Deferred income taxes as a liability discussed**

Chapter 15, FRA 3.

Chapter 15, FRA 4.

1.

2.

Chapter 15, FRA 5.

(amounts in millions except per share data):

Toys "R" Us:

Book Value per Share	=	
2002	=	
	=	
2001	=	
	=	

Average market stock price 4th quarter of 2001 =

Walgreens:

Book Value per Share	=	
2002	=	
	=	
2001	=	
	=	

Average market stock price 4th quarter of 2002 =

Discussion:

Chapter 15, FRA 5.

Chapter 16, SE 1.

1.
2.
3.
4.
5.

Chapter 16, SE 2.

20x4				
Apr.	1			

Chapter 16, SE 3.				
20xx Mar.	1	Cash		

Chapter 16, SE 4.		
Choice A		
Present value of 40 periodic payments at 6%		
Total present value of Choice A		
Choice B		
Present value of 30 periodic payments at 6%		
Total present value of Choice B		
Total present value of both bonds		

Chapter 16, SE 5.

a.	Sept.	1			

Chapter 16, SE 6.

Entries prepared in journal form

20xx Sept.	1			

Bond interest expense calculated

Chapter 16, SE 7.

20x4				
Oct.	1			

Chapter 16, SE 8.

Dec.	1				

Chapter 16, SE 9.

20x5					
Mar.	1				

Chapter 16, SE 10.

Month	Monthly Payment	Interest for 1 Month at .6667%* on Unpaid Balance	Reduction in Debt	Unpaid Balance at End of Period
0				
1				
2				
3				

Chapter 16, E 1.

	Interest Coverage Ratio	=	
	20x4	=	
		=	
	20x5	=	
		=	

Comments:

Chapter 16, E 2.

20x4				
Feb.	1			

Chapter 16, E 3.

20x5				

Chapter 16, E 4.

20xx				

Chapter 16, E 5.

20x4					

Chapter 16, E 6.

Choice A

Choice B

Chapter 16, E 7.

a.	Present value of 20 periodic payments at 5%	
	Issue price (total present value) of bond issue	
b.	Present value of 20 periodic payments at 3%	
	Issue price (total present value) of bond issue	
c.	Present value of 20 periodic payments at 4%	
	Issue price (total present value) of bond issue	
d.	Present value of 40 periodic payments at 6%	
	Issue price (total present value) of bond issue	
e.	Present value of 40 periodic payments at 3%	
	Issue price (total present value) of bond issue	

Chapter 16, E 8.

Face value of 30-year, 10% zero coupon bonds, compounded annually:
  Present value of a single payment at the end of 30 periods at 10%

  Face value =

Face value of 50-year, 10% zero coupon bonds, compounded annually:
  Present value of a single payment at the end of 50 periods at 10%

  Face value =

Face value of 30-year, 8% zero coupon bonds, compounded annually:
  Present value of a single payment at the end of 30 periods at 8%

  Face value =

Face value of 50-year, 8% zero coupon bonds, compounded annually:
  Present value of a single payment at the end of 50 periods at 8%

  Face value =

Chapter 16, E 9.

2006					

Chapter 16, E 10.

a.	Sept.	1			

Chapter 16, E 11.

1. Entries prepared in journal form

20xx			

2. Bond interest expense calculated

Chapter 16, E 12.

20x3			

Chapter 16, E 13.

1. Current market value of the bonds calculated

Issue price (total present value) of bond issue	

2. Retirement of the bonds recorded

Chapter 16, E 14.

Sept.	1			

Chapter 16, E 15.

20x8 July	1			

Chapter 16, E 16.

1. Monthly payment schedule prepared

Month	Monthly Payment	Interest for 1 Month at 1% on Unpaid Balance	Reduction in Debt	Unpaid Balance at End of Period
0				
1				
2				
3				

*Rounded.

2. Entries prepared in journal form

Month 0			
Month 1			
Month 2			

Chapter 16, E 17.

1. Present value calculated

2. Entry to record the lease agreement prepared in journal form

3. Entry to record depreciation for the first year prepared in journal form

4. Entries to record lease payments prepared in journal form

Year 1

Year 2

Chapter 16, P 1.

1. Entries for bonds issued at more than face value prepared in journal form

Chapter 16, P 1. (Continued)

2. Entries for bonds issued at less than face value prepared in journal form

Chapter 16, P 1. (Continued)

3. Entries for bonds issued at face value plus accrued interest prepared in journal form

Chapter 16, P 2.

1. Entries for bonds issued at more than face value prepared in journal form

Chapter 16, P 2. (Continued)

2. Entries for bonds issued at less than face value prepared in journal form

Chapter 16, P 2. (Continued)

3. Entries for bonds issued at face value plus accrued interest prepared in journal form

Chapter 16, P 3.

20x4				

Chapter 16, P 3. (Continued)

20x4				

Chapter 16, P 4.

1. Bond interest and discount amortization table prepared

Semi-annual Interest Period	A Carrying Value at Beginning of Period	B Semiannual Interest Expense at 5% to Be Recorded* (5% × A)	C Semiannual Interest Payment to Bondholders (4-1/2% × $60,000,000)	D Amortization of Discount (B − C)	E Unamortized Bond Discount at End of Period (E − D)	F Carrying Value at End of Period (A + D)
0					$2,659,200	$57,340,800
1						
2						
3						
4						
5						
6						
7						
8						
9						
10						
11						
12						

*Rounded to the nearest dollar.

2. Calculate loss on early retirement of one-half of bonds payable on July 1, 20x4

Chapter 16, P 5.

20x3

Chapter 16, P 5. (Continued)

20x4				

Chapter 16, P 5. (Continued)

20x5					

Chapter 16, P 6.

1. Entries for bonds issued at more than face value prepared in journal form

Mar.	1			

2. Entries for bonds issued at less than face value prepared in journal form

Chapter 16, P 6. (Continued)

3. Entries for bonds issued at face value plus accrued interest prepared in journal form

June	1			

Chapter 16, P 7.

1. Entries for bonds issued at more than face value prepared in journal form

Date				
June	1			

Chapter 16, P 7. (Continued)

2. Entries for bonds issued at less than face value prepared in journal form

June	1			

Chapter 16, P 7. (Continued)

3. Entries for bonds issued at face value plus accrued interest prepared in journal form

Aug.	1			

Chapter 16, P 8.

20x3				

Chapter 16, P 8. (Continued)

20x3				

Chapter 16, SD 1.

Chapter 16, SD 2.

Chapter 16, SD 3.

Chapter 16, SD 4.

Chapter 16, SD 6.

Memorandum

To:
From:
Date:
Re:

Chapter 16, FRA 1.

Chapter 16, FRA 2.

Chapter 16, FRA 3.

Interest Coverage Ratio =

(in millions of yen)

NEC		Sanyo	
2001	2000	2001	2000

Comments:

Chapter 16, FRA 4.

1.

2.

Chapter 16, FRA 5.

(dollars in millions)

Toys "R" Us's Debt to Equity Ratio:

Debt to Equity =

2002:

2001:

Toys "R" Us's Interest Coverage Ratio

Interest Coverage Ratio =

2002:

2001:

Chapter 16, FRA 5. (Continued)

(dollars in millions)

Walgreens' Debt to Equity Ratio:

Debt to Equity =

2002:

2001:

Walgreens' Interest Coverage Ratio

Interest Coverage Ratio =

2002:

2001:

Evaluation and comments:

Chapter 17, SE 1.

1.		4.	
2.		5.	
3.		6.	

Chapter 17, SE 2.

Cash Flow Yield	=	
	=	
Cash Flows to Sales	=	
	=	
Cash Flows to Assets	=	
	=	
Free Cash Flow	=	
	=	
	=	

Chapter 17, SE 3.

Chapter 17, SE 4.

Global Market Corporation
Schedule of Cash Flows from Operating Activities
For the Year Ended December 31, 20x4

Chapter 17, SE 5.

Cheng Corporation
Schedule of Cash Flows from Operating Activities
For the Year Ended December 31, 20x4

Chapter 17, SE 6.

Schedule of Noncash Investing and Financing Transactions

Chapter 17, SE 7.

Chapter 17, SE 8.

1.	5.
2.	6.
3.	7.
4.	8.

Chapter 17, E 1.

1.	6.	11.
2.	7.	12.
3.	8.	13.
4.	9.	
5.	10.	

Chapter 17, E 2.

Cash Flow Yield =

=

Cash Flows to Sales =

=

Cash Flows to Assets =

=

Free Cash Flow =

=

=

Chapter 17, E 3.

Gro-More Chem Company
Schedule of Cash Flows from Operating Activities
For the Year Ended December 31, 20x4

Cash flows from operating activities		
Net income		$600,000

Chapter 17, E 4.

Germaine Corporation
Schedule of Cash Flows from Operating Activities
For the Year Ended December 31, 20x5

Cash flows from operating activities		
Net income		$41,000

Chapter 17, E 5.

Pine Corporation
Schedule of Cash Flows from Operating Activities
For the Year Ended June 30, 20xx

Cash flows from operating activities		
Net income		$ 7,400

Chapter 17, E 6.

Cash flows from investing activities		

The net cash flow from the sale is computed as follows:

Chapter 17, E 7.

Cash flows from investing activities

The cash inflow from the disposal was:

Chapter 17, E 8.

Schedule of Noncash Investing and Financing Transactions

Chapter 17, E 9.

Margol Corporation
Statement of Cash Flows
For the Year Ended June 30, 20x5

Cash flows from operating activities

Cash flows from investing activities

Schedule of Noncash Investing and Financing Transactions

Chapter 17, P 1.

	Cash Flow Classification				Effect on Cash Flows		
Transaction	Operating Activity	Investing Activity	Financing Activity	Noncash Transaction	Increase	Decrease	No Effect
1. Incurred a net loss.	X					X	
2. Declared and issued a stock dividend.							
3. Paid a cash dividend.							
4. Decreased accounts receivable.							
5. Increased inventory.							
6. Retired long-term debt with cash.							
7. Sold available-for-sale securities at a loss.							
8. Issued stock for equipment.							
9. Decreased prepaid insurance.							
10. Purchased treasury stock with cash.							
11. Retired a fully depreciated truck (no gain or loss).							
12. Increased interest payable.							
13. Decreased dividends receivable on investment.							
14. Sold treasury stock.							
15. Increased income taxes payable.							
16. Transferred cash to money market account.							
17. Purchased land and building with a mortgage.							

Chapter 17, P 2.

1. Statement of cash flows prepared

Maron Corporation
Statement of Cash Flows
For the Year Ended December 31, 20x5

Schedule of Noncash Investing and Financing Transactions

Chapter 17, P 2. (Continued)

2. Causes of increase in cash identified

3. Computation and assessment of cash flow yield and free cash flow

Cash Flow Yield	=	
	=	
Free Cash Flow	=	
	=	
	=	

Chapter 17, P 3.

1. Statement of cash flows prepared

Pierre Fabrics, Inc.
Statement of Cash Flows
For the Year Ended December 31, 20x5

Schedule of Noncash Investing and Financing Transactions

Chapter 17, P 3. (Continued)

2. Causes of increase in cash identified

3. Computation and assessment of cash flow yield and free cash flow

Cash Flow Yield	=	
	=	
Free Cash Flow	=	
	=	
	=	

Chapter 17, P 4.

1. Statement of cash flows prepared

Maggio Masonry, Inc.
Statement of Cash Flows
For the Year Ended December 31, 20x5

Schedule of Noncash Investing and Financing Transactions

Chapter 17, P 4. (Continued)

2. Causes of decrease in cash identified

3. Computation and assessment of cash flow yield and free cash flow

Cash Flow Yield	=	
	=	
Free Cash Flow	=	
	=	
	=	

Chapter 17, P 5.

Transaction	Cash Flow Classification					Effect on Cash Flows		
	Operating Activity	Investing Activity	Financing Activity	Noncash Transaction		Increase	Decrease	No Effect
1. Earned a net income.	X					X		
2. Declared and paid a cash dividend.								
3. Issued stock for cash.								
4. Retired long-term debt by issuing stock.								
5. Increased accounts payable.								
6. Decreased inventory.								
7. Increased prepaid insurance.								
8. Purchased a long-term investment with cash.								
9. Sold trading securities at a gain.								
10. Sold a machine at a loss.								
11. Retired fully depreciated equipment.								
12. Decreased interest payable.								
13. Purchased available-for-sale securities (long-term).								
14. Decreased dividends receivable.								
15. Decreased accounts receivable.								
16. Converted bonds to common stock.								
17. Purchased 90-day Treasury bill.								

Chapter 17, P 6.

1. Statement of cash flows prepared

Sulyat Corporation
Statement of Cash Flows
For the Year Ended June 30, 20x7

Schedule of Noncash Investing and Financing Transactions

Chapter 17, P 6. (Continued)

2. Causes of increase in cash identified

3. Computation and assessment of cash flow yield and free cash flow

Cash Flow Yield	=	
	=	
Free Cash Flow	=	
	=	
	=	

Chapter 17, P 7.

1. Statement of cash flows prepared

Fernandez Fashions, Inc.
Statement of Cash Flows
For the Year Ended December 31, 20x6

Schedule of Noncash Investing and Financing Transactions

Chapter 17, P 7. (Continued)

2. Causes of increase in cash identified

3. Computation and assessment of cash flow yield and free cash flow

Cash Flow Yield	=	
	=	
Free Cash Flow	=	
	=	
	=	

Chapter 17, SD 1.

Chapter 17, SD 4.

1. Statement of cash flows prepared

Hashimi Print Gallery, Inc.
Statement of Cash Flows
For the Year Ended December 31, 20x4

Schedule of Noncash Investing and Financing Transactions

Chapter 17, SD 4. (Continued)

2. Cash problem explained

Chapter 17, FRA 1.

1. Make required computations and label the document "Attachment"

Attachment

All dollar amounts are in millions.

Cash Flow Yield =

    2001: =

    2000: =

Cash Flows to Sales =

    2001: =

    2000: =

Cash Flows to Assets =

    2001: =

    2000: =

Free Cash Flow =

    2001: =

    2000: =

Chapter 17, FRA 1. (Continued)

2. Prepare a memorandum to the investment analyst

Memorandum

Date:
To:
From:
Re:

Chapter 17, FRA 2.

Sony:	Canon:

Cash Flow Yield =

1999:

2000:

Cash Flows to Sales =

1999:

2000:

Cash Flows to Assets =

1999:

2000:

Free Cash Flow =

1999:

2000:

Discussion:

Chapter 17, FRA 3.

1.

2.

3.

Chapter 17, FRA 4.

(dollars in millions)

Toys "R" Us's cash flow yield:

Cash Flow Yield =

2002:

2001:

Toys "R" Us's cash flow to sales ratio:

Cash Flows to Sales Ratio =

2002:

2001:

Toys "R" Us's cash flow to assets ratio:

Cash Flows to Assets Ratio =

2002:

=

2001:

=

Toys "R" Us's free cash flow:

Free Cash Flow =

2002:

2001:

Chapter 17, FRA 4. (Continued)

(dollars in millions)

Walgreens' cash flow yield:

Cash Flow Yield =

2002:

2001:

Walgreens' cash flow to sales ratio:

Cash Flows to Sales Ratio =

2002:

2001:

Walgreens' cash flow to assets ratio:

Cash Flows to Assets Ratio =

2002:

=

2001:

=

Walgreens' free cash flow:

Free Cash Flow =

2002:

2001:

Chapter 17, FRA 4. (Continued)

Chapter 18, SE 1.

1.
2.
3.
4.
5.

Chapter 18, SE 2.

1.
2.
3.
4.
5.

Chapter 18, SE 3.

	20x6	20x5	20x4
Net sales			
Accounts receivable (net)			

Comments:

Chapter 18, SE 4.

SiteWorks, Inc.
Comparative Income Statements
For the Years Ended December 31, 20x5 and 20x4

	20x5	20x4	Increase or Decrease Amount	Percentage
Net sales	$180,000	$145,000		
Cost of goods sold	112,000	88,000		
Gross margin	$ 68,000	$ 57,000		
Operating expenses	40,000	30,000		
Operating income	$ 28,000	$ 27,000		
Interest expense	7,000	5,000		
Income before income taxes	$ 21,000	$ 22,000		
Income taxes	7,000	8,000		
Net income	$ 14,000	$ 14,000		
Earnings per share	$ 1.40	$ 1.40		

Comments:

Chapter 18, SE 5.

SiteWorks, Inc.
Common-Size Balance Sheets
December 31, 20x5 and 20x4

Assets	20x5	20x4
Liabilities and Stockholders' Equity		

Comments:

Chapter 18, SE 6.

	20x5			20x4		
Current ratio:						
Quick ratio:						
Receivable turnover:						
Average days' sales uncollected:						

(continued)

Chapter 18, SE 6. (Continued)

	20x5			20x4		
Inventory turnover:						
Average days' inventory on hand:						
Payables turnover:						
Average days' payable:						

Chapter 18, SE 7.

	20x5	20x4
Profit margin:		
Asset turnover:		
Return on assets:		
Return on equity:		

Comment:

Chapter 18, SE 8.

	20x5		20x4	
Debt to equity ratio:				
Interest coverage ratio:				

Comment:

Chapter 18, SE 9.

	20x5	20x4
Cash flow yield:		
Cash flows to sales:		
Cash flows to assets:		
Free cash flow:		
Comment:		

Chapter 18, SE 10.

	20x5	20x4
Price/earnings ratio:		
Dividends yield:		
Comment:		

Chapter 18, E 1.

1.	5.
2.	6.
3.	7.
4.	

Chapter 18, E 2.

<table>
<tr><th colspan="5">Trumpet Company
Comparative Balance Sheets
December 31, 20x4 and 20x3</th></tr>
<tr><th></th><th>20x4</th><th>20x3</th><th colspan="2">Increase or Decrease</th></tr>
<tr><th></th><th></th><th></th><th>Amount</th><th>Percentage</th></tr>
<tr><td>**Assets**</td><td></td><td></td><td></td><td></td></tr>
<tr><td>Current assets</td><td>$ 37,200</td><td>$ 25,600</td><td></td><td></td></tr>
<tr><td>Property, plant, and equipment (net)</td><td>218,928</td><td>194,400</td><td></td><td></td></tr>
<tr><td>Total assets</td><td>$256,128</td><td>$220,000</td><td></td><td></td></tr>
<tr><td>**Liabilities and Stockholders' Equity**</td><td></td><td></td><td></td><td></td></tr>
<tr><td>Current liabilities</td><td>$ 22,400</td><td>$ 6,400</td><td></td><td></td></tr>
<tr><td>Long-term liabilities</td><td>70,000</td><td>80,000</td><td></td><td></td></tr>
<tr><td>Stockholders' equity</td><td>163,728</td><td>133,600</td><td></td><td></td></tr>
<tr><td>Total liabilities and stockholders' equity</td><td>$256,128</td><td>$220,000</td><td></td><td></td></tr>
</table>

Comment:

Chapter 18, E 3.

	20x7	20x6	20x5	20x4	20x3
Net sales					
Cost of goods sold					
General and administrative expenses					
Operating income					

Comment:

Chapter 18, E 4.

Trumpet Company
Common-Size Income Statements
For the Years Ended December 31, 20x6 and 20x5

	20x6	20x5
Net sales		
Cost of goods sold		
Gross margin		
Selling expenses		
General expenses		
Total operating expenses		
Operating income		

Comment:

Chapter 18, E 5.

	20x4	20x3
Current ratio		
Quick ratio		
Receivable turnover		
Average days' sales uncollected		
Inventory turnover		
Average days' inventory on hand		
Payables turnover		
Average days' payable		

Comment:

Chapter 18, E. 6.

Year	Receivable Turnover		Payables Turnover		Inventory Turnover	
20x1:						
20x2:						
20x3:						
20x4:						

Comment:

Chapter 18, E 7.

	20x5			20x4		
Profit margin						
Asset turnover						
Return on assets						
Return on equity						

Comment:

Chapter 18, E 8.

	Company M		Company N	
Debt to equity ratio				
Interest coverage ratio				
P/E ratio				
Dividends yield				
Comment:				

Chapter 18, E 9.

Cash flow yield	
Cash flows to sales	
Cash flows to assets	
Free cash flow	

Chapter 18, P 1.

1. Schedules showing amount and percentage changes prepared

Rochelle Corporation
Comparative Income Statements
For the Years Ended December 31, 20x5 and 20x4

	20x5	20x4	Increase (Decrease) Amount	Increase (Decrease) Percentage
Net sales	$1,600,800	$1,485,200		
Costs and expenses				
Cost of goods sold	$ 908,200	$ 792,400		
Selling expenses	260,200	209,200		
Administrative expenses	280,600	231,000		
Total costs and expenses	$1,449,000	$1,232,600		
Income from operations	$ 151,800	$ 252,600		
Interest expense	50,000	40,000		
Income before income taxes	$ 101,800	$ 212,600		
Income taxes	28,000	70,000		
Net income	$ 73,800	$ 142,600		
Earnings per share	$1.23	$2.38		

Chapter 18, P 1. (Continued)

Rochelle Corporation
Comparative Balance Sheets
December 31, 20x5 and 20x4

	20x5	20x4	Increase or Decrease Amount	Percentage
Assets				
Cash	$ 62,200	$ 54,400		
Accounts receivable (net)	145,000	85,400		
Inventory	245,200	215,600		
Property, plant, and equipment (net)	1,155,400	1,015,000		
Total assets	$1,607,800	$1,370,400		
Liabilities and Stockholders' Equity				
Accounts payable	$ 209,400	$ 144,600		
Notes payable	100,000	100,000		
Bonds payable	400,000	220,000		
Common stock, $10 par value	600,000	600,000		
Retained earnings	298,400	305,800		
Total liabilities and stockholders' equity	$1,607,800	$1,370,400		

Chapter 18, P 1. (Continued)

2. Common-size income statements and balance sheets prepared

Rochelle Corporation
Common-Size Income Statements
For the Years Ended December 31, 20x5 and 20x4

	20x5	20x4
Net sales		
Costs and expenses		
Cost of goods sold		
Selling expenses		
Administrative expenses		
Total costs and expenses		
Income from operations		
Interest expense		
Income before income taxes		
Income taxes		
Net income		

Rochelle Corporation
Common-Size Balance Sheets
December 31, 20x5 and 20x4

	20x5	20x4
Assets		
Cash		
Accounts receivable (net)		
Inventory		
Property, plant, and equipment (net)		
Total assets		
Liabilities and Stockholders' Equity		
Accounts payable		
Notes payable		
Bonds payable		
Common stock, $10 par value		
Retained earnings		
Total liabilities and stockholders' equity		

Chapter 18, P 1. (Continued)

3. Results commented on

Chapter 18, P 2.

	Transaction	Ratio	Effect		
			Increase	Decrease	None
a.	Issued common stock for cash.				
b.	Declared cash dividend.				
c.	Sold treasury stock.				
d.	Borrowed cash by issuing note payable.				
e.	Paid salaries expense.				
f.	Purchased merchandise for cash.				
g.	Sold equipment for cash.				
h.	Sold merchandise on account.				
i.	Paid current portion of long-term debt.				
j.	Gave sales discount.				
k.	Purchased marketable securities for cash.				
l.	Declared 5% stock dividend.				
m.	Purchased a building.				

Chapter 18, P 3.

Ratio	20x5	20x4	Favorable (F) or Unfavorable (U) Change
1. Liquidity analysis			
a. Current ratio			
b. Quick ratio			
c. Receivable turnover			
d. Average days' sales uncollected			
e. Inventory turnover			
f. Average days' inventory on hand			
g. Payables turnover			
h. Average days' payable			

Note: All amounts used in calculating the ratios and percentages are in thousands of dollars except the amounts used to calculate the PE ratio and the dividends yield.

Chapter 18, P 3. (Continued)

Ratio	20x5	20x4	Favorable (F) or Unfavorable (U) Change
2. Profitability analysis			
a. Profit margin			
b. Asset turnover			
c. Return on assets			
d. Return on equity			
3. Long-term solvency analysis			
a. Debt to equity ratio			
b. Interest coverage ratio			

Note: All amounts used in calculating the ratios and percentages are in thousands of dollars except the amounts used to calculate the PE ratio and the dividends yield.

(continued)

Chapter 18, P 3. (Continued)

Ratio	20x5	20x4	Favorable (F) or Unfavorable (U) Change
4. Cash flow adequacy analysis			
a. Cash flow yield			
b. Cash flows to sales			
c. Cash flows to assets			
d. Free cash flow			
5. Market strength analysis			
a. Price/earnings ratio			
b. Dividends yield			

Chapter 18, P 3. (Continued)

6. Evaluation of Rochelle's performance

Liquidity:

Profitability:

Long-term solvency:

Cash flow adequacy:

Summary:

Chapter 18, P 4.

Ratio	Reynard	Bouche
1. Liquidity analysis		
a. Current ratio		
b. Quick ratio		
c. Receivable turnover		
d. Average days' sales uncollected		
e. Inventory turnover		
f. Average days' inventory on hand		
g. Payables turnover		
h. Average days' payable		

(continued)

Chapter 18, P 4. (Continued)

Ratio	Reynard	Bouche
2. Profitability analysis		
a. Profit margin		
b. Asset turnover		
c. Return on assets		
d. Return on equity		
3. Long-term solvency analysis		
a. Debt to equity ratio		
b. Interest coverage ratio		

(continued)

Chapter 18, P 4. (Continued)

Ratio	Reynard	Bouche
4. Cash flow adequacy analysis		
a. Cash flow yield		
b. Cash flows to sales		
c. Cash flows to assets		
d. Free cash flow		
5. Market strength analysis		
a. Price/earnings ratio		
b. Dividends yield		

Chapter 18, P 4. (Continued)

6. Comparative analysis

	Ratio Name	Reynard	Bouche	Company with More Favorable Ratio
1.	Liquidity analysis			
	a. Current ratio			
	b. Quick ratio			
	c. Receivable turnover			
	d. Average days' sales uncollected			
	e. Inventory turnover			
	f. Average days' inventory on hand			
	g. Payable turnover			
	h. Average days' payable			
2.	Profitability analysis			
	a. Profit margin			
	b. Asset turnover			
	c. Return on assets			
	d. Return on equity			
3.	Long-term solvency analysis			
	a. Debt to equity ratio			
	b. Interest coverage ratio			
4.	Cash flow adequacy analysis			
	a. Cash flow yield			
	b. Cash flows to sales			
	c. Cash flows to assets			
	d. Free cash flow			
5.	Market strength analysis			
	a. Price/earnings ratio			
	b. Dividends yield			

7. Use of information from prior years

Chapter 18, P 5.

	Transaction	Ratio	Effect		
			Increase	Decrease	None
a.	Sold merchandise on account.				
b.	Sold merchandise on account.				
c.	Collected on accounts receivable.				
d.	Wrote off an uncollectible account.				
e.	Paid on accounts payable.				
f.	Declared cash dividend.				
g.	Incurred advertising expense.				
h.	Issued stock dividend.				
i.	Issued bonds payable.				
j.	Accrued interest expense.				
k.	Paid previously declared cash dividend.				
l.	Purchased treasury stock.				
m.	Recorded depreciation expense.				

Chapter 18, P 6.

Ratio	20x6	20x5	Favorable (F) or Unfavorable (U) Change
1. Liquidity analysis			
a. Current ratio			
b. Quick ratio			
c. Receivable turnover			
d. Average days' sales uncollected			
e. Inventory turnover			
f. Average days' inventory on hand			
g. Payables turnover			
h. Average days' payable			

(continued)

Chapter 18, P 6. (Continued)

Ratio	20x6	20x5	Favorable (F) or Unfavorable (U) Change
2. Profitability analysis			
a. Profit margin			
b. Asset turnover			
c. Return on assets			
d. Return on equity			
3. Long-term solvency analysis			
a. Debt to equity ratio			
b. Interest coverage ratio			

(continued)

Chapter 18, P 6. (Continued)

Ratio	20x6	20x5	Favorable (F) or Unfavorable (U) Change
4. Cash flow adequacy analysis			
a. Cash flow yield			
b. Cash flows to sales			
c. Cash flows to assets			
d. Free cash flows			
5. Market strength analysis			
a. Price/earnings ratio			
b. Dividends yield			

Chapter 18, P 6. (Continued)

6. Evaluation of Lisle's performance

Liquidity:

Profitability:

Long-term solvency:

Cash flow adequacy:

Summary:

Chapter 18, SD 1.

Chapter 18, SD 2.

Based on Exhibit 1, Goodyear's business segments are:

The relative size of the segments in terms of sales and income for 2002 ar as follows (amounts in millions):

Segment	Sales		Income	
	Amount	Percentage	Amount	Percentage
Totals				

Discussion:

Chapter 18, SD 3.

Memorandum

Date:
To:
From:
Re:

Chapter 18, SD 4.

Chapter 18, SD 6.

1. Common-size income statements, profit margin, and return on equity

	Apple a Day	Unforgettable Edibles
Net sales		
Cost of goods sold		
Gross margin		
Operating expenses		
Operating income		
Gain on sale of real estate		
Interest expense		
Income before income taxes		
Income taxes		
Net income (profit margin)		
Return on equity		

2. Results discussed

Chapter 18, SD 6. (Continued)

Chapter 18, FRA 1.

Summary of operations	2001	2000	1999	1998	1997
Sales					
Cost of products sold					
Interest expense					
Provision for income taxes					
Net income (before special items)					
Other related data					
Dividends paid: Common					
Total assets					
Total debt					
Shareholders' equity					

Discussion:

Chapter 18, FRA 2.

	Pfizer	Roche
Receivable turnover		
Average days' sales uncollected		
Inventory turnover		
Average days' inventory on hand		
Payables turnover		
Average days' payable		
Operating cycle		
Days of financing required		

Comparison of results:

Chapter 18, FRA 3.

All computations are for the years ended February 3, 2000, and February 2, 2001 (in millions).

Liquidity ratios and analysis of Toys "R" Us

	2002	2001
Current ratio		
Quick ratio		
Receivable turnover		
Average days' sales uncollected		
Inventory turnover		
Average days' inventory on hand		
Payables turnover		
Average days' payable		

Comment:

Chapter 18, FRA 3. (Continued)

Profitability ratios and analysis of Toys "R" Us

	2002	2001
Profit margin		
Asset turnover		
Return on assets		
Return on equity		

Comment:

Chapter 18, FRA 3. (Continued)

Long-term solvency ratios and analysis of Toys "R" Us

	2002	2001
Debt to equity ratio		
Interest coverage ratio		

Comment:

Cash flow adequacy ratios and analysis of Toys "R" Us

	2002	2001
Cash flow yield		
Cash flows to sales		
Cash flows to assets		
Free cash flow		

Comment:

Chapter 18, FRA 3. (Continued)

Market strength ratios and analysis of Toys "R" Us

	2002	2001
Price/earnings ratio		
Dividends yield		

Comment:

Chapter 18, FRA 4.

Toys "R" Us and Walgreens compared across key financial performance measures

	Toys "R" Us		Walgreens	
	2002	2001	2002	2001
Liquidity:				
Operating cycle				
Days of financing needed				
Profitability:				
Profit margin				
Asset turnover				
Return on assets				
Long-term solvency:				
Debt to equity				
Cash flow adequacy:				
Cash flow yield				
Free cash flow				

Chapter 18, FRA 4. (Continued)

Liquidity ratios of Walgreens

	2002	2001
Receivable turnover		
Average days' receivable		
Inventory turnover		
Average days' inventory on hand		
Payables turnover		
Average days' payable		

Discussion:

Liquidity:

Profitability:

Long-term solvency:

Cash flow adequacy:

Chapter 18, FRA 4. (Continued)

Profitability ratios of Walgreens

	2002	2001
Profit margin		
Asset turnover		
Return on assets		

Long-term solvency ratios of Walgreens

Debt to equity		

Cash flow adequacy ratios of Walgreens

Cash flow yield		
Free cash flow		

APPENDIX A — INTERNATIONAL ACCOUNTING

Appendix A, P 1.

Part A:

Part B:

Date				
Nov.	15			

Appendix A, P 2.

Aug.	12			

Appendix A, P 2. (Continued)

APPENDIX B   LONG-TERM INVESTMENTS

Appendix B, P 1.

1.
   Reason:

2.
   Reason:

3.
   Reason:

4.
   Reason:

5.
   Reason:

6.
   Reason:

Appendix B, P 2.

20x4				

Appendix B, P 2. (Continued)

20x5				

Appendix B, P 3.

1. Entries in journal form prepared

Quarter 1			

Appendix B, P 3. (Continued)

2. T account prepared

Investment in Vivanco Company

APPENDIX C THE TIME VALUE OF MONEY

Appendix C, E 1.

(1) Simple interest

(2) Compounded semiannually

(3) Compounded quarterly at 3% for 4 periods

(4) Compounded monthly at 1% for 12 periods

Appendix C, E 2.

(1) Single payment of $20,000 at 7% for 10 years

(2) Ten annual payments of $2,000 at 7%

(3) Single payment of $6,000 at 9% for 7 years

(4) Seven annual payments of $6,000 at 9%

Appendix C, E 3.

(1) Compounded annually

(2) Compounded semiannually at 4% for 14 periods

(3) Compounded quarterly at 2% for 28 periods

Appendix C, E 4.

(1) 10% compounded annually

(2) 10% compounded semiannually

Year	Balance		Rate		Interest	Deposits
1		x		=		
1		x		=		
2		x		=		
2		x		=		
3		x		=		
3		x		=		
4		x		=		
4		x		=		
End of year 4						

(3) 4% compounded annually

Appendix C, E 4. (Continued)

(4) 16% compounded quarterly

Year	Balance		Rate		Interest	Deposits
1		x		=		
1		x		=		
1		x		=		
1		x		=		
2		x		=		
2		x		=		
2		x		=		
2		x		=		
3		x		=		
3		x		=		
3		x		=		
3		x		=		
4		x		=		
4		x		=		
4		x		=		
4		x		=		
End of year 4						

Appendix C, E 5.

a. Required rate of return, $20,000 invested, $40,000 needed in 12 years

To find table factor, for use with Table 1 in the appendix on future value and present value tables:

To find interest rate for which table factor after 12 years equals 2.000:

Rate	Factor

Required rate of return is _____

b. Time required for $40,000 at 7% to accumulate to $64,000

To find table factor, for use with Table 1 in the appendix on future value and present value tables:

To find number of periods for which table factor at 7% equals 1.600:

Periods	Factor

Pruitt must wait _____ years to buy his summer home.

Appendix C, E 6.

Table factor for the amount of $1 paid in each period, for 4 years at 8%:

Appendix C, E 7.

Saber should expect to pay

Appendix C, E 8.

(1)

(2)

(3)

(4)

Appendix C, E 9.

	Years	Rate	Factor from Table ___*				Present Value of $60,000
(1)				x		=	
(2)				x		=	
(3)				x		=	
(4)				x		=	

Appendix C, E 10.

	Payments	Rate	Factor from Table ___*				Present Value of $1,200 Payments
(1)				x		=	
(2)				x		=	
(3)				x		=	
(4)				x		=	

*In the appendix on future value and present value tables.

Appendix C, E 12.

Present value of the purchase transaction:

Appendix C, E 13.

Future payment	x		=	Present Value	
	x		=		

The entries necessary to record the purchase and subsequent payment in Borst's records are as follows:

Jan.	1			
Oct.	1			

Appendix C, E 13. (Continued)

The entries necessary to record the sale and subsequent receipt in Johnson's records are as follows:

Jan.	1			
Oct.	1			

Appendix C, E 14.

	x		=	Future Value	
	x		=		

Jan.	1			
Feb.	1			
Mar.	1			

Appendix C, E 15.

	÷		=	
	÷		=	

Journal entry:

Appendix C, E 16.

Raftson's offer to sell:

From Table 4 in the appendix on future value and present value tables:

	X		=	
	X		=	

Ruiz's offer to buy:

From Table 4 in the appendix on future value and present value tables:

	X		=	
	X		=	

| The range between the offer to sell and the offer to buy is from: | | to |

Account Name	Trial Balance		Adjustments		Adjusted Trial Balance		Income Statement		Balance Sheet	
	Debit	Credit	Debit	Credit	Debit	Credit	Debit	Credit	Debit	Credit

Work Sheet (continued)

Account Name	Trial Balance		Adjustments		Adjusted Trial Balance		Income Statement		Balance Sheet	
	Debit	Credit	Debit	Credit	Debit	Credit	Debit	Credit	Debit	Credit

Work Sheet

Account Name	Trial Balance		Adjustments		Adjusted Trial Balance		Income Statement		Balance Sheet	
	Debit	Credit	Debit	Credit	Debit	Credit	Debit	Credit	Debit	Credit

Work Sheet (continued)

Account Name	Trial Balance		Adjustments		Adjusted Trial Balance		Income Statement		Balance Sheet	
	Debit	Credit	Debit	Credit	Debit	Credit	Debit	Credit	Debit	Credit

Date	Description	Post. Ref.	Debit	Credit

Date	Description	Post. Ref.	Debit	Credit

General Journal — Page

Date	Description	Post. Ref.	Debit	Credit

General Journal — Page

Date	Description	Post. Ref.	Debit	Credit

General Ledger

Date	Item	Post. Ref.	Debit	Credit	Balance Debit	Balance Credit

Date	Item	Post. Ref.	Debit	Credit	Balance Debit	Balance Credit

General Ledger

Date	Item	Post. Ref.	Debit	Credit	Balance Debit	Balance Credit

Date	Item	Post. Ref.	Debit	Credit	Balance Debit	Balance Credit

General Ledger

Date	Item	Post. Ref.	Debit	Credit	Balance Debit	Balance Credit

Date	Item	Post. Ref.	Debit	Credit	Balance Debit	Balance Credit

Date	Item	Post. Ref.	Debit	Credit	Balance Debit	Balance Credit

Date	Item	Post. Ref.	Debit	Credit	Balance Debit	Balance Credit

Date	Item	Post. Ref.	Debit	Credit	Balance Debit	Balance Credit

General Ledger

Date	Item	Post. Ref.	Debit	Credit	Balance Debit	Balance Credit

Date	Item	Post. Ref.	Debit	Credit	Balance Debit	Balance Credit

Date	Item	Post. Ref.	Debit	Credit	Balance Debit	Balance Credit

Date	Item	Post. Ref.	Debit	Credit	Balance Debit	Balance Credit

Date	Item	Post. Ref.	Debit	Credit	Balance Debit	Balance Credit